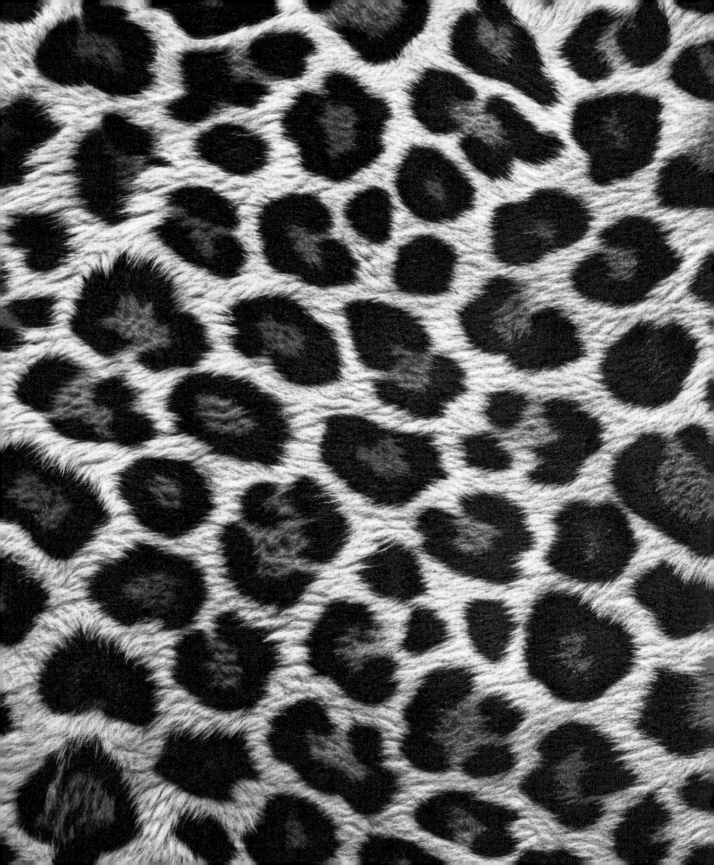

If These Walls Could Talk

CARMEL PHILLIPS

TEN PEAKS PRESS®
EUGENE, OR

FOR BRAD,
Home is wherever I'm with you.
FOR COLLIN AND JOSIE,
You will forever be my inspiration.

Contents

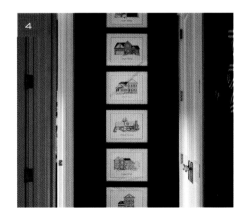

Introduction

D ecorating has not always been a passion of mine, but I have always loved to read. While I could not have cared less about the floral wallpaper on my childhood bedroom walls (Was it cream with pink flowers or pink with cream flowers?), I spent hours absorbing every detail of Green Gables alongside Anne Shirley. (How sad were those whitewashed bare walls? At least she could see the cherry tree in full bloom from her window.) It honestly was not until I had a home of my own that I started to pay attention to the actual rooms in which I was reading. Without a doubt, my love for a beautiful setting has shaped my design ethos. For me, home is more than just the place where we live; it's the setting of our life story.

It was my story-centric design philosophy that led me to start my DIY design blog, *Our Fifth House*, back in 2010, shortly after we moved into our *fifth* house–genius, right? This little corner of the internet is where I continue to share my decorating adventures, even though we are now living in our *seventh* house. Clearly, I've moved a lot (and should have put a little more thought into naming my blog, but I digress).

In each house my family has called home, I have learned something new about decorating. While I'm certainly not an expert or a hardcore do-it-yourselfer, practice, lots of trial and error, and a fearless attitude have allowed me to hone my personal design vibe and truly lean into my heart-forward way of decorating. From the very beginning of my interest in design, I have believed that flipping the narrative on what our homes mean to us has an important impact on the way we go about decorating them. We often hear, *Home is where the heart is.* Yes. True. But saying, *Home is the setting of our life story*—that's a game changer! When we view home in such a significant way, suddenly decorating becomes so much more . . . *meaningful, personal, and important.* Because we're thinking not just of how we want home to look but of how we want home to *feel.* Decorating *matters.* Our homes are the backdrop of our lives. They will color our memories forever. How do we want them to be remembered?

Creating unique spaces filled with personality is my passion, and I love encouraging others to do the same in their homes. What you will not find in these pages is a list of decorating dos and don'ts. Rather, this book is your permission slip to let your creativity run free, and it is a road map to curating a home that speaks to your unique design vibe. I hope my practical decorating advice bolsters your confidence, gives you a fresh perspective, and leaves you feeling inspired to create spaces in which you love to live. After all, an empty room is a story just waiting to happen, and *you* get to be the author. If the walls in your home could talk, what would you want them to say?

Home is
the setting
of our
life story.

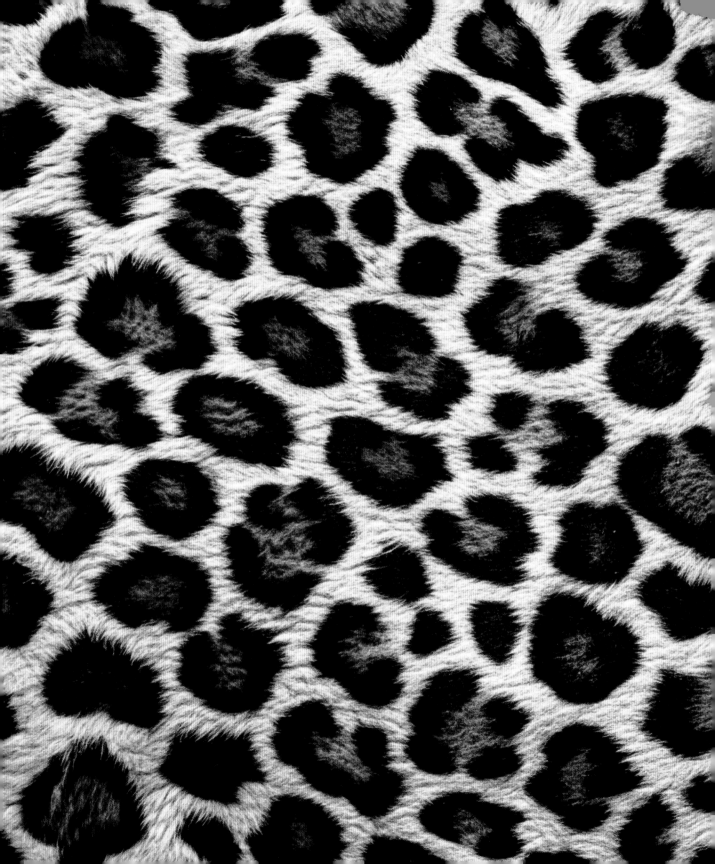

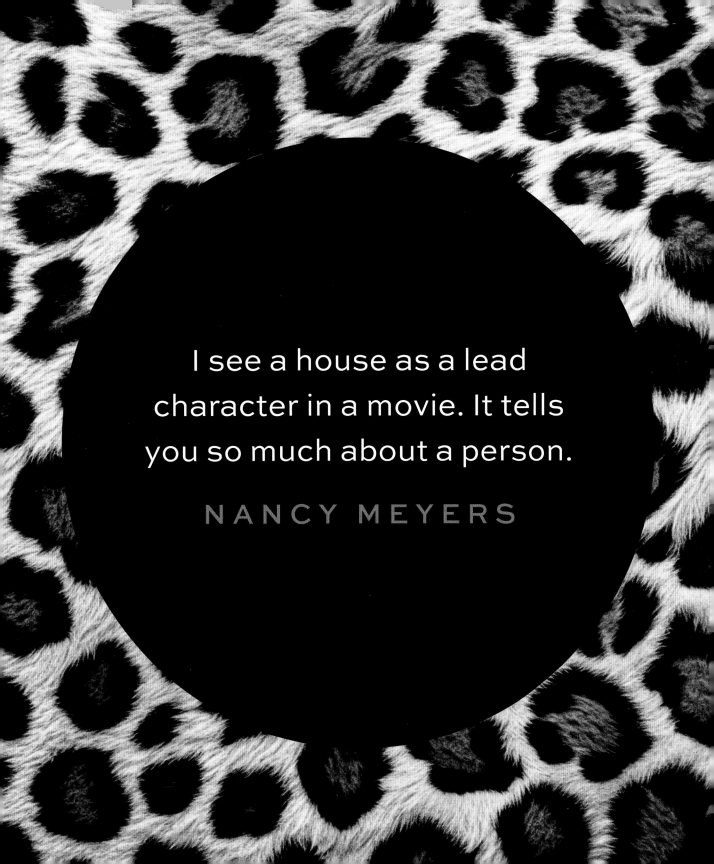

I see a house as a lead character in a movie. It tells you so much about a person.

NANCY MEYERS

CHAPTER ONE

Discovering Your Unique Style

As a twentysomething, newly married, first-time homeowner just beginning to decorate her first house, I struggled to define my design style. I took every "find your decor style" quiz I came across and somehow ended up with a different result every time. So many hours were spent watching decorating television shows, and yet the only decorating idea that really hit home was a cautionary tale—never staple silk flowers to the wall. If you know, you know. In all seriousness, though, every designer on *Trading Spaces* gave me the confidence to play with decorating ideas in my home, and for that I will be eternally grateful. I mean, the floral-explosion bathroom designed by Hildi Santo-Tomas may still live in my mind rent-free, but I will always believe fearlessness in design should not be underestimated. It should be applauded!

While describing my design style using typical categories was challenging, I did not let that stop me from experimenting with different looks. And well, let's just say, my first homes reflected my design identity crisis. To say that I'm grateful there is no online photographic evidence of the first two places my husband and I called home is the understatement of my life. But my family and closest friends regularly love to teasingly remind me of my quite humble design beginnings.

Honestly, though, I'm grateful for those years that included lots of crackle paint, a frog prince cookie jar, a neon yellow laundry room, and a vintage radio flyer wagon I used as a living-room side table. Bless. My. Heart. My design identity crisis era was wild, friends! Mistakes were made. Lessons were learned.

What is the best lesson I learned during that time? Finding your design *vibe* trumps finding your design *style*. When I threw out the idea of *labeling the look* and leaned into *describing the feel* I was after, that was the light bulb moment for me. That is when it all started to come together, and I finally found my design rhythm.

Finding Your Vibe

Even if you can confidently define your design style, I think focusing on your design vibe is helpful. It allows you to drive home your decorating style in a more purposeful way. Design styles can be a great jumping-off point. However, it can be tricky to try to fit into one box or mesh a lot of different styles to create spaces that are truly a reflection of who you are. What I have found is that focusing on the vibe, the mood, or the feeling I want my home to convey—rather

My design identity crisis era was wild, friends! Mistakes were made. Lessons were learned.

than the way I want my spaces to look—allows me to hone a style that is uniquely my own.

Trends in the world of interior design are ever evolving. Shabby Chic was all the rage when I was a twentysomething. Just a few years ago, the modern farmhouse style was exploding on Instagram, and as I draft this book, Grandmillenial style is making a huge splash. While there is nothing wrong with playing with trends or owning your design style, finding your design *vibe* gives you the insight to make your style timeless, personal, and one of a kind. It is less *copy and paste*, and more *be inspired and create, cultivate, and curate*.

Do you identify or feel at home with one or a few of these typical design styles?

Traditional	Modern	Bohemian	Maximalist
Minimalist	Coastal	Shabby Chic	French Country
English Cottage	Farmhouse	Rustic	Neo-Industrial
Eclectic	Midcentury Modern	Cottagecore	Transitional
Contemporary	Modern Farmhouse	New Traditional	Regency

Blissful
Bold
Bright
Calm
Casual
Cheerful
Comfortable
Cozy
Dignified
Dramatic
Energetic
Flirty
Fun
Gleeful
Happy
Joyful
Lively
Moody
Nostalgic
Peaceful
Playful
Quirky
Relaxing
Romantic
Serene
Tranquil
Vibrant
Vivacious
Warm
Whimsical
Zany

There is no wrong answer here, in case you are feeling nervous. If you feel confident declaring your design style, that can be wonderfully helpful when you are decorating your home. I would say, if I'm forced to choose a few of the typical design style words to simplify things, I would probably call my style Eclectic Transitional. I like mixing traditional elements with modern, but I also like sprinkling in coastal and midcentury modern touches. Is your head spinning? Welcome to my design brain. It can be a little nutty in there. While I'm slightly better at describing my style now, I didn't really have the language to describe the look I was after until I found my design *vibe*.

A Quick *Homework* Assignment

So, how do you do that? How exactly do you find your design vibe? It's simple. There are no quizzes involved. Just one simple question: How do you want your home to *feel*? The answer to that question is your vibe. Don't think too hard. Quickly, grab a pencil and a notebook. What words immediately come to mind? How do you want your home to feel when you get back after a long day? How do you want visitors to feel when they are in your home?

Does one or more of these words at left describe how you want your home to feel?

It is more than okay if the words you would use to describe the vibe you want for your home are not on this list. This collection of words is just meant to get you thinking in terms of feelings instead of styles. I recommend choosing three main words to describe the overall vibe you want for your home. And as you reflect on each individual room in your home, you might land on one or two

alternates. Your alternate words will replace one of your three words to better describe the vibe you want for that particular room.

Fashion influencer and wardrobe consultant Allison Bornstein (https://www.allisonbornstein.com) recommends choosing three words to describe your fashion style. With fashion and home design both providing the perfect opportunity to express your individual style, it comes as no surprise that this exercise works well in both arenas.

As an example, my design vibe words for my home are: *warm*, *bold*, and *comfortable*. And my alternate words are: *moody* and *whimsical*. Warm and bold are my staples. This is the vibe I want every room in my house to convey, but comfortable is interchangeable in some spaces. I have replaced comfortable with moody or whimsical in a few rooms. My powder room, for instance, is not a space where comfort was top of mind. Whimsical better describes the specific vibe I wanted to create in that space. So, the overall look feels warm, bold, and whimsical. The vintage brass and wood plant stands bring warmth, while the color of the walls paired with the black-and-white tile design feels bold. And the art, chandelier, and metallic wallpaper on the ceiling bring in a whimsical vibe.

Could I describe this space as Modern Traditional? Maybe. But leaning into my design vibe—warm, bold, and whimsical—is what helped me bring this space to life. Is this a space everyone is going to like? No. But everyone does not live in my home, so everyone's opinion does not matter. I'm not trying to convince you to like my design vibe. My goal is to encourage you to find yours.

QUICK TIP

When going through this quick design exercise, it can also be helpful to identify how you *don't* want your home to feel. Maybe you don't want your home to feel stuffy, formal, or fussy. Identifying how you don't want your home to feel can be as helpful as identifying how you do want it to feel.

Why three words? Because threes work well in design (more on that in chapter 7). But honestly, you do not have to choose three words. I have found, though, that the mix of three words seems to magically create a design vibe that is utterly personal and unique.

Take a Cue from Your Wardrobe

If you are struggling to answer the question of how you want your home to feel, take a field trip. You will not have to go far; you do not even need to leave your home. The answer to that question is likely lurking in your dresser drawers and your closet. Let your wardrobe be your guide. What you feel at home wearing is often a great indicator of what you will feel at home surrounding yourself with when it comes to decorating.

Do you live in jeans and t-shirts? Casual and comfortable might be your staple design vibe words. Is your closet filled with floral prints and dresses? Romantic comes to mind. Do you get the most excited about sweater season? Warm and cozy sounds like you. The answers are there. Maybe you didn't realize it but, more often than not, what excites you in the fashion world translates to interior design.

Warm, autumnal colors make up the majority of my wardrobe, and I've rarely met a leopard print I did not love. Hello, **bold**. While I spend most of my days in tennis shoes, a glittery heel makes me feel things. So, welcome to the show, **comfortable** and **whimsical**. Finally, my favorite band is The Cure, and if I am not wearing red, camel, or burnt orange, I'm in black. And **moody** just entered the chat. Moral of the story? Take a cue from your wardrobe.

QUICK TIP

If you are still unsure after looking through your wardrobe, ask a trusted friend how they would describe your fashion vibe. Sometimes we do not see ourselves as accurately as others do because we can be overly self-critical.

Striped Door

Painting the back of a door makes for a fun surprise in a powder room! Stripes are classic and timeless, but when done in bold colors, they can feel whimsical. Paired with a glass doorknob, they bring in an Alice in Wonderland flair.

SUPPLIES NEEDED

–Two different paint colors (I used the colors Plum Dandy and Chinese Red in a semi-gloss Sherwin-Williams Emerald Urethane Trim Enamel)

–Fine-grit sandpaper

–Smooth surface paint roller

–Level

–Delicate surface painter's tape (emphasis on *delicate surface*)

STEP-BY-STEP PROCESS

Step 1: Lightly sand to prep the door for the base paint color.

Step 2: Using a smooth surface paint roller, apply your chosen base color.

Step 3: Allow the base to cure (fully dry) before taping. Then use a level to carefully place your first stripe of tape. The first one is the most important. Once that one is in place, you will build off it, placing a small piece of tape next to your taped stripe to use as a guide as you work from top to bottom taping off the next stripe. Continue this process until the entire door is completely striped with tape.

Step 4: Gently press down the edges of your tape before painting your second color to prevent the paint from bleeding through.

Step 5: Carefully remove tape before the paint has completely dried to avoid peeling the paint.

QUICK TIP

A small craft paintbrush works well for any needed touch-ups.

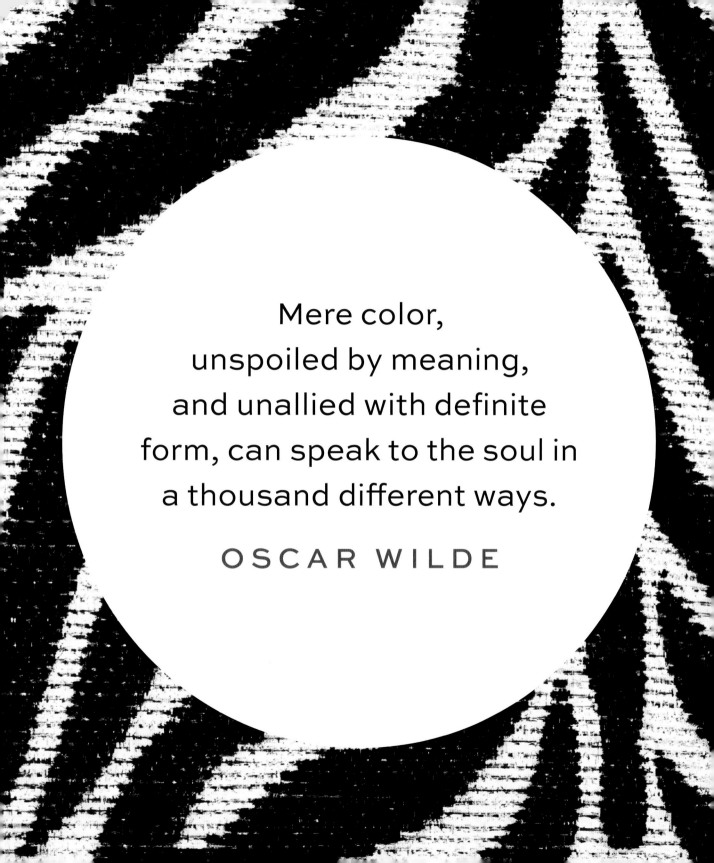

Mere color,
unspoiled by meaning,
and unallied with definite
form, can speak to the soul in
a thousand different ways.

OSCAR WILDE

CHAPTER TWO

Using Paint to Color Your Home's Mood

Nothing has more of an impact on the vibe of a space than color! This is why I love paint so much. The very first paint color I ever rolled onto walls myself was Ralph Lauren's Hunting Coat Red, and it has been a love story ever since. The power of paint just cannot be beaten. For me, standing in front of the paint swatch wall at my local hardware store is the grown-up version of opening a fresh, new box of crayons. The endless color possibilities feel so exciting and inspiring. However, I know a lot of people find themselves standing in front of that same giant wall of paint swatches feeling uncertain and intimidated.

I wrote this chapter especially for you—for you who are nervous to pick a paint color or afraid you are going to choose the "wrong" color. I wrote this for you who are not quite sure how to transition paint colors in your home. For those who always stick to neutrals because they feel "safe," I hope this chapter brings you clarity and gets you excited to play with paint. I mean, there is certainly nothing wrong with neutral walls (I have quite a few white walls in my own home). However, if it is fear or doubt that is holding you back from coloring the walls, ceilings, moldings, or furniture in your home with shades that speak to you and convey your unique style and personality, I hope this chapter boosts your confidence. I want to encourage you to start selecting paint colors with enthusiasm and intention as God, the greatest designer of all, intended.

Nothing has more of an impact on the vibe of a space than color!

Without question, paint is the most impactful and easily accessible design tool you can use to color your home's mood. It can make a room feel open and airy, cozy and inviting, or vibrant and cheerful. And I believe, as with any tool, a few tips and tricks can help you wield it fearlessly.

Without question, paint is the most impactful and easily accessible design tool you can use to color your home's mood.

The Psychology of Color in Design

My guess is when you think about paint colors in terms of decorating your home, you think about how colors will look. I am going to encourage you to stop thinking that way. Instead, I want you to focus on the *vibe* that different colors bring into a space. Color psychology in interior design is the school of thought that focuses on setting a mood

and creating an atmosphere with the intention of invoking a particular emotional response. It flips our conventional thinking and encourages us to reflect on how colors make us *feel*. Next time you visit a friend's house, patronize a restaurant, or stay in a hotel, consider how you feel in those spaces and take a mental note of the colors being used.

In our vocabulary, we have been using color to paint our moods for centuries. Seeing red, having the blues, being tickled pink, feeling green with envy—our feelings around colors are intrinsic. Do you remember how old you were when you first proudly declared your favorite color? My guess is that your age was in the single digits. Tapping into your core color instincts will help you to start thinking about the emotions colors evoke for you and can help you feel more confident when making color selections for your home.

In general, according to color psychology:

red—warm, stimulating color that feels courageous and passionate

orange—vibrant color that demands attention and feels warm and cheerful

yellow—color associated with joy and optimism, it feels sunny and happy

green—drawing on nature, it brings the outside in and feels peaceful and refreshing

blue—reminds us of the sky, feels calming and tranquil

purple—associated with royalty, it feels luxurious and dramatic

pink—a softer tint from the red family, it feels romantic and nurturing

brown—tied to nature, represents earth, feels comfortable and warm

black—makes a bold statement that feels dramatic and mysterious

grey—a versatile neutral that feels productive and minimalist

white—creates a blank canvas, feels fresh and clean

The way color influences us may differ depending on many variables including age, gender, and culture. And while I have focused on the positive feelings colors can evoke, they can evoke negative emotions in us as well. The way we perceive color is deeply personal. Shades of grey that one person may find calming another person might find depressing. There are colors that one person may absolutely love while another person could never even imagine wanting to use them. Sir Isaac Newton may have established color theory when he invented the color wheel in 1666, but only *you* inherently know if red excites you or scares you or if blue calms you or bores you.

Colors can make us feel relaxed or energized, cheerful or gloomy, peaceful or frenzied. And while the psychology of color is fascinating, the gap between creating a mood with color and actually selecting paint colors for your home can still feel a bit daunting. Even when we can confidently say we love certain colors, we can still feel some trepidation over choosing paint colors to use in our homes. This is exactly why I am such a huge advocate for creating a whole home color palette.

Three Easy Steps for Creating a Whole Home Color Palette

Creating a color palette for your whole home takes a little time and research, but it is so worthwhile. And not to be dramatic, but having a home color palette is a game changer when it comes to selecting paint colors for each room in your home. If nothing else, my hope is that my three-step process for creating your home's color palette will boost your paint-color-selecting confidence.

And not to be dramatic, but having a home color palette is a game changer when it comes to selecting paint colors for each room in your home.

If terms like *complementary*, *analogous*, and *monochromatic* sound foreign to you, do not fret. Contrary to what you may have heard on the topic, I believe selecting the "right" colors for your home is actually more about personal preference than it is about your knowledge of the color wheel or the rooms you are selecting colors for.

Reflect on Your Design Vibe

Before you head to the paint store, circle back to chapter 1, and spend some time reflecting on your design vibe. The words you used to describe how you want your home to *feel* are an important part of the paint selection process. If you have not already, write them down. Because color is such a powerful design tool when it comes to making your home feel a particular way, describing the feeling you want each of the rooms in your home to convey is vital to selecting your home's color palette.

Once you have your design vibe words written down, you can then start to consider what colors you feel match the vibe you want to create.

- Do you want your home to feel welcoming, creative, and cheerful? You may want to lean towards colors that are light, bright, and clear.
- Does luxurious, elegant, and distinguished sound more like you? Colors that are cool and intense might be more your speed.
- Are you going for more of a cozy, romantic vibe in your home? Maybe try soft, muted shades.

Because color sets the mood, reflecting on your design vibe words is the perfect place to start when creating a whole home color palette.

Your design vibe acts as a funnel as it begins to narrow down the endless color possibilities.

Find Your Inspiration Piece

Your inspiration piece can be anything you *love* that fits your design vibe. It can be an old painting you cherish, a favorite art print, a scrap of fabric or wallpaper, or even a vintage rug. Whatever your inspiration piece is, having something to use as a jumping-off point makes creating a coordinating color palette for your whole home so much easier as it gives you a road map to help you find your way in the paint store.

This step is all about helping you bring your design vibe to life and curating a palette of colors that coordinate well with one another.

And yes, this is more homework, but it is absolutely worth the effort. Once you know your vibe, finding your inspiration piece helps to further narrow down your options. If describing your vibe is a funnel, think of finding your inspiration piece as a strainer.

Your inspiration piece will become your personal color guide.

QUICK TIP

Keep a picture of your inspiration piece on your phone, so you always have it with you to use as reference. It will come in handy for everything from selecting paint colors and choosing fabrics to shopping for decor accessories.

Start with a Paint Color Collection or Use an Online Color Generator

Now that you have nailed down your design vibe and found your inspiration piece, you are ready to head to the paint store. Rather than staring blankly at the wall of a million paint swatches, go directly to the paint color *collections*. Most paint brands put together

collections of paint colors in beautiful brochures that include not only the paint swatches but also a few pictures of rooms that have been painted with the featured colors.

These paint color collections feature harmonious colors that are perfect for creating a palette of colors for your home that will flow effortlessly from room to room. Because they have already done the work of curating colors that coordinate well with one another, selecting your home's paint colors from a collection like this takes a great deal of the guesswork out of creating a whole home color palette.

However, if you are unable to find a collection that speaks to your vibe and represents your inspiration piece, technology can be your best friend. Nowadays, most paint companies' websites offer online tools that allow you to upload a picture of your inspiration piece so you can generate a coordinating palette of paint colors in mere seconds.

My Home's Color Palette

Of course, I used my own three-step process when I was creating the color palette for my current home. Going for a **warm, bold, comfortable,** *sometimes* **moody** or **whimsical** design vibe, I chose to use a deeply saturated, colorful vintage rug that lives in my walk-in pantry as my inspiration piece. This led me straight to the Colors of Historic Charleston

Paint Color Collection by Duron for Sherwin-Williams. This collection perfectly captured the vibe I was after and represented the colors in my inspiration piece. Almost every paint color in my home has come from the Historic Charleston Paint Color Collection.

The paint colors that did not come from that collection still coordinate very well because the beauty of creating a whole home color palette is that once you have even just a few colors selected, finding other paint colors that coordinate with your chosen palette is much simpler. Finding a paint color collection or using an online paint generator tool based on your inspiration piece acts as a springboard to help you create your home's unique paint color collection. And because you started by creating a palette of coordinating paint colors for your home rather than choosing just one paint color, you are already on your way to effortless design flow in your home.

Using Paint to Create Design Flow

Design flow makes every room in a home feel connected. The goal is for every room, like individual puzzle pieces, to fit together to tell one design story. And color, via paint especially, acts as a great tool to visually tie spaces together. You can absolutely create design flow using a medley of bold paint colors, allowing each space to feel unique yet still cohesive.

And creating a whole home color palette does make this almost effortless, but one way I like to visually connect spaces with paint is to use the wall color in one space as an accent color in another. This trick is especially helpful

The goal is for every room, like individual puzzle pieces, to fit together to tell one design story.

when spaces are within view of one another, such as in open-concept floor plans. My walk-in pantry's walls, cabinets, shelving, ceiling, and glass door are all painted light blue (Hurricane Blue), and the island in my attached kitchen is painted the same color blue, as is the ceiling in my dining room. All three spaces in my open-concept home look and feel different and special in their own way yet are visually connected by this one shade of blue.

The 60-30-10 Rule

While I am not a huge fan of rules when it comes to decorating, I do think the 60-30-10 rule of thumb can be especially helpful for creating a cohesive design story with color. With this decorating method, you will need three colors: a base or main color, a secondary color, and an accent color. Your base color will take up about 60 percent of the room. The secondary color will take up about 30 percent, and your accent color 10 percent. Then to create design flow, in the next room you will alter the percentages of these colors. As an example, here are the colors in my butler's pantry and adjoining kitchen:

BUTLER'S PANTRY	KITCHEN
Base Color – Blue	Base Color – White
Secondary Color – Red	Secondary Color – Blue
Accent Color – White	Accent Color – Red

Color Repetition Is Not a Bad Thing

Repeating colors throughout a home helps to visually tie rooms together, and it is a trick I have personally used a few times in my home. My closet walls, shelves, and ceiling were painted with the same pink paint color as the exterior of our home. Why continue to reinvent the wheel? Especially when repeating colors not only reduces paint color decision fatigue but also creates continuity throughout a home.

Let us say, for instance, you want to paint your powder room red, and your front door is already a shade of red you really love. Why not use the same red paint color? It creates continuity when you repeat paint colors in different spaces and in diverse ways throughout a home.

Because every room receives light differently, paint colors do not appear the exact same way in every space. So even if you do choose to use the same wall color in different rooms, your spaces will not feel overly redundant but rather more connected.

I used the same green (Tradd Street Green) for the walls in both my husband's office and my son's bedroom. While the wall color is the same, these rooms feel quite different. One room receives morning light while the other is drenched with sunlight in the late afternoon. One room is on the main level and the other is upstairs. The green wall color visually connects these rooms in our home, yet it does not feel too repetitive. In my husband's office, everything but the ceiling is green, whereas in my son's bedroom I left most of the trim white. The rooms feel related but not identical. The key to making repeating colors interesting instead of boring is

Repeating colors throughout a home helps to visually tie rooms together.

QUICK TIP

Keep in mind that you can have a paint color reduced (lightened) at the paint store for a slightly less saturated look. So, if a color is a bit too intense or vibrant for you, reducing it by about 25 percent will decrease the pigment.

intentionality. Making sure there are enough design differences in the rooms to keep them from looking too similar creates a compelling, cohesive design story.

The Fifth Wall

Why should walls get all the love? The ceiling, or what I like to refer to as *the fifth wall*, is unfortunately an all too often neglected blank canvas. However, the color of your ceiling plays such a significant role in the overall vibe of a room that it most definitely should not be an afterthought. A colorfully painted ceiling can make such a bold, unique statement! As a bonus, a painted ceiling can provide a wonderful way to create design flow in a home.

I like to think of the ceiling as the cherry on top of a sundae. Painted ceilings not only liven up a space and add personality to the overall design, but they can visually play with the proportions of a room as well. In a smaller room with lightly colored walls, painting the ceiling a dark color draws the eye up, making the walls appear taller, thereby making the space feel grander and more spacious. Whereas in a large room, a dark ceiling color visually brings the ceiling down and makes the space feel cozier.

Ceilings are most often painted in flat finishes. However, a satin or glossy finish offers a reflective quality, bouncing light back down into a space. In rooms that do not see much natural light, this reflective effect can brighten the space.

QUICK TIP

If you are going to use anything other than a flat finish paint on your ceiling, keep in mind that higher-sheen finishes will highlight any surface flaws. So, you will want your ceiling to be perfectly smooth and blemish-free before painting. In addition, you may want to hire a professional painter if you are not going to use a flat finish. Painting ceilings with reflective finishes can be tricky for the novice or even intermediate do-it-yourselfer.

While a boldly colored ceiling makes a dramatic design statement, a classic white ceiling will always hold its rightful place in design. After all, the eye needs a place to rest. A bright white ceiling offsets a bold wall color perfectly and makes the ceiling appear higher. In rooms with white or light neutral-toned walls, white ceilings blend with the walls and visually expand the space, creating an open, airy vibe. In rooms lacking natural light, white ceilings reflect whatever small amount of light is available.

There is no doubt white ceilings will always be in style. But personally, I love to use a shade of blue on the ceiling! It replicates the sky. Cliché, I know, but this always adds an unexpected, whimsical yet classic design element to a space. Black is another favorite choice of mine for a ceiling, especially in hallways. A black ceiling adds the perfect punch of drama to the other often-neglected space in a home, the hallway.

I will generally advocate for painting a ceiling in a statement-making color! Why? Because painting a ceiling is one of the easiest, quickest, and most inexpensive ways to breathe new life into a space. Even in a large room, painting a ceiling takes hardly any time at all. And unless you are using a reflective paint sheen, painting a ceiling is a beginner-friendly do-it-yourself project. It adds depth, contrast, and interest, especially in a room with neutral walls. The beauty of paint is it is so easily changed. When or if you tire of a color, you can simply roll right over it with something different. So why not go for bold?!

QUICK TIP

In a room with white walls, if you are not going to use a contrasting paint color for the ceiling, use the same white paint color on your ceiling. When different shades of white are next to each other, one often looks dingy.

Color Drenching

Drenching an entire room in one color is my favorite way to bring drama to a space. No matter what vibe you are after in a space or what color you choose to use, painting the walls, trim work, doors, and ceiling all the same color (a.k.a. color drenching) makes a high-impact, visually stunning design statement. The bonus is color drenching is a budget-friendly way to make a room look larger.

The Design Paint Trick That Makes Rooms Look Larger

Regardless of whether you choose a light or dark paint color, painting the ceiling the same color as the walls makes it look and feel larger. Using paint in this way is the closest thing to a magic trick in design. It draws the eye up and creates the illusion of a higher ceiling, thereby making your space feel grander and appear larger. This is a brilliant design trick to play in any space, but especially in rooms that lack either square footage or high ceilings. Keep in mind, this trick will only work if the trim work, more specifically the crown molding, is painted the same color as the walls and ceiling. The key to this design paint trick is in keeping the color *seamless*. With no stopping point or visual breaking point for the color, the ceiling appears to recede, tricking the eye and making the space feel larger than it is.

QUICK TIP

Something to consider when selecting a paint color for a ceiling is a ceiling naturally casts its own shadow, so whatever paint color you choose will appear slightly darker on the ceiling than on the wall.

From a do-it-yourself perspective, the benefit to color drenching is not having to cut in or tape off the ceiling. While you will want to use a higher-sheen finish on the trim work, when you are using the same paint color any mistakes, even with different sheens, will be far less noticeable.

Using paint in this way is the closest thing to a magic trick in design.

Moody, Daring, or Romantic?

While an all-one-color space makes an impression, the mood or vibe created depends on the color you choose. A room drenched in a deep, bold color feels dramatic and daring, while a space wrapped in a bright, vibrant color feels daring and fun. Color drenching with a pale or muted shade can usher in a romantic, understated elegance. Soft, seamless color has a way of creating a restful, calming vibe in a space. You can take the color drenching one step further by including the furniture in a room as well.

QUICK TIP

Since ceilings cast their own shadows, have the color reduced by 20 to 30 percent if you are using the same color on the walls and ceiling. This way the ceiling paint (though a slightly lighter shade) will appear to be the same color tone as the full-strength paint color on the walls.

Painted Furniture

We have focused mostly on walls and ceilings—for good reason—but painted furniture can also be a powerful tool when setting the mood in a space. Brightly painted pieces bring in a cheerful, happy vibe while those painted in soft, muted shades add a casual, cozy feel to a room. Painted furniture can either make a bold statement or can blend in with the decor of the room, all depending on your chosen hue. A coat of paint often breathes new life into a piece that no longer excites you, allowing you to appreciate it once more, seeing it with a fresh perspective.

Certainly not all furniture needs a coat of paint. The natural array of brown, red, and blonde tones in raw wood absolutely add warmth and interest to a space. But painting furniture provides an opportunity to play with color in smaller doses, allowing you the freedom to use colors you may not necessarily want to use to blanket an entire room. In addition, selecting a paint color for a piece of furniture rather than the walls or ceiling of a room can feel like a lower-stakes design decision. With the pressure off, you can enjoy the freedom to play and experiment with paint colors. And this can boost your paint-color-selecting confidence!

QUICK TIP

Circling back to the 60-30-10 rule, painted furniture provides a straightforward way to create design flow in a home. The side table in my bedroom was painted the same shade of red as the striped door in my powder room and the dresser in my closet. Picking up on the red wallpaper in my laundry room and red accents in my kitchen and pantry, this painted side table brings in an intentional pop of red color that calls back to other spaces in our home.

Painting Furniture to Match Your Walls

In the same way that rooms painted all one color trick the eye, creating the illusion of a larger space, painting a piece of furniture to match your walls can make the piece visually disappear. A tone-on-tone furniture look reduces visual clutter and makes rooms appear more spacious. This look not only feels uber-chic, but it is a useful design trick to pull out in smaller spaces where you want to create the appearance of more square footage. The effect of a tone-on-tone furniture makeover is visually calming yet anything but boring.

No matter what color you choose, painting a piece of furniture is an easy, beginner-friendly DIY project. And the bonus is you do not have to be a DIY expert, nor do you need to own a fancy paint sprayer to achieve a great result.

Two Painted Furniture Makeovers Featuring My Two Favorite Paints

Over the years, I have used many different paints for a variety of furniture makeovers. With zero hesitation, my two favorite types of paint to use on furniture are chalk paint and enamel paint.

Both paints are easy to work with, even for the novice, delivering beautiful results using simple tools like paintbrushes and rollers. Which paint is preferable? It depends greatly on the specific piece of furniture you are painting and your desired result.

Chalk Paint:

- Minimal prep work—priming and/or sanding rarely needed
- Great option for a distressed finish
- Often requires sealing with a wax or top coat
- Matte or eggshell finish
- Range of colors depends on brand

Enamel Paint:

- Typical prep work required—sanding and/or priming
- Provides a hard, durable finish
- A top coat is optional
- High gloss, semi-gloss, or satin finish
- Can most often be color matched to your desired shade

I prefer chalk paint when painting pieces like chairs and furniture with carved, ornate detailing since it most often does not require any sanding before applying the paint and yet still provides excellent adhesion even without the use of a primer. For pieces that have large, flat surfaces, like tables and dressers, I typically opt to use an enamel paint, as it delivers an exceptionally durable, wipeable, smooth, and completely brushstroke-free finish. While I do not have a favorite brand of chalk paint, my go-to for enamel paint is Sherwin-Williams' Emerald Urethane Trim Enamel (which I love to use not only for furniture but also for painting trim work).

Four-Poster Bed Makeover
with Chalk Paint

A few years ago, I gave our old mahogany four-poster bed a fresh look in classic black. With its carved details, I opted to take advantage of the minimal prep work required (no sanding) that chalk paint offers.

SUPPLIES NEEDED

–Furniture cleaner/degreaser
–Lint-free rag
–Short-handled angled paintbrush
–6-inch high-density foam roller
–Paint tray

–Chalk paint (I used Velvet Finishes in black)
–Polycrylic Protective Finish (Clear Satin) by Minwax

STEP-BY-STEP PROCESS

Step 1: Start with a thorough cleaning using a cleaner/degreaser and a lint-free rag. This step is meant to de-gloss the surface for the best paint adhesion. Your furniture piece should have a completely flat finish before you begin applying the paint.

Step 2: Apply chalk paint using a short-handled angled brush for any furniture details and a 6-inch foam roller for the flat surface areas. Chalk paint dries fast, so it is best to work in small sections, allowing the paint to dry completely before applying a second coat.

Step 3: Once the paint is completely dry, apply an even coat of the Polycrylic protective finish.

QUICK TIP

For the smoothest finish, be sure to use a high-density foam roller as opposed to any other kind of roller that could leave a stipple finish (an orange peel–like texture).

QUICK TIP

For optimal results when painting a piece of furniture, it is important that each coat of paint dries thoroughly before the application of another coat of paint.

Dresser Makeover
with Enamel Paint

When I decided to paint this dresser in my closet a bright, glossy red, I just knew I had to go with my favorite paint from Sherwin-Williams, Emerald Urethane Trim Enamel. This enamel paint delivers an incredible finish every time! It looks like I used a paint sprayer, but a simple paint brush and roller produced these results.

SUPPLIES NEEDED

–Household cleaning spray and lint-free rag

–Fine-grit sandpaper

–6-inch foam roller and tray

–Kilz Premium primer

–Enamel paint with gloss finish (I used Sherwin-Williams Emerald Urethane Trim Enamel in Chinese Red)

–Short-handled angled paintbrush

STEP-BY-STEP PROCESS

Step 1: Start with a thorough cleaning.

Step 2: Lightly sand with a fine-grit sandpaper.

Step 3: Apply a light coat of Kilz Premium primer. This is a fast-drying, stain-blocking, low VOC, water-based primer that provides excellent adhesion. It is formulated to hide imperfections to prepare surfaces for painting.

Step 4: After allowing the primer to dry thoroughly, use a paintbrush and foam roller to apply Emerald Urethane Trim Enamel. For the smoothest results, apply light coats and allow the paint to dry completely between each coat of paint.

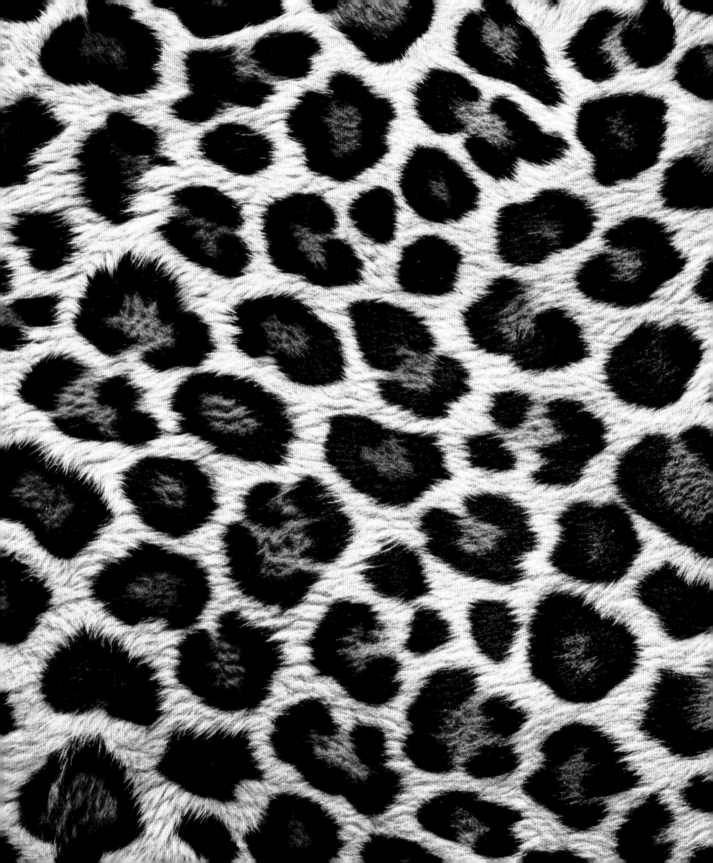

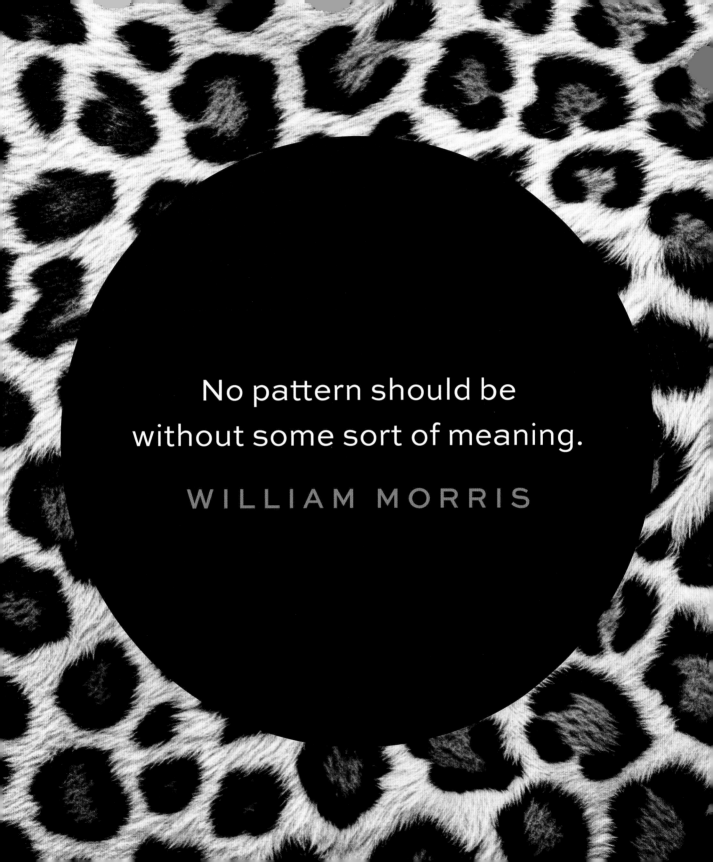

No pattern should be
without some sort of meaning.

WILLIAM MORRIS

CHAPTER THREE

Playing with Pattern to Add Flair

Pattern is the spice in design. It's what adds flair and flavor to a home. Where color sets the mood, pattern adds personality!

Like color, pattern is a powerful design tool that can also invoke an array of emotions. It breathes life into a room and further sets the tone in a home. From bold, geometric prints that bring in an energetic vibe to feminine florals that add a soft layer of cozy romance, patterns add interest, style, and texture to spaces. And there are so many great ways to infuse pattern into a room. From tile, wallpaper, and furniture to rugs, window treatments, and throw pillows, the opportunities are truly endless.

While I have never shied away from using color in my home, incorporating patterns in my interiors used to be my biggest design hurdle. Mixing patterns felt very intimidating to me, so for years I stuck to solids because they felt safe. I would then wonder why I was never quite happy with my finished spaces. It was like I was making a pot of chili and was afraid to use chili powder and red pepper. My fear of adding spice to my interiors left my rooms feeling flavorless and flat. The thing is, you never really know just how much spice you can handle until you try it. Just like the best homemade chilis that keep the recipe loose with no exact measurements—just a handful of this and a pinch of that—the magic in using pattern in a home is in seeing it as a playground rather than a puzzle. There is something about the idea of playing with patterns that feels a lot more fun, too. When I let go of the fear of getting it wrong, I realized that getting it right was actually pretty simple!

There is no doubt that solids play a vital role in design, and we will discuss their importance later in this chapter. However, if you resonate with how I used to feel and find yourself shying away from incorporating patterns into your home's decor, my hope is that this chapter helps you tap into your creativity and unlock your pattern-loving, print-mixing self, so that you can soar over this design hurdle in your home as well. Based on my personal approach to playing with patterns in my home, I have pulled together some tips and ideas. However—spoiler alert!—we will not be discussing any design *rules*. Actually, I take that back. The most important rule is the only rule I will be sharing: There are no rules!

When you throw out the rules and the mere idea of a right or a wrong way to go about mixing patterns, your creativity has room to flourish. When your creativity is given the space and the freedom

The magic in using pattern in a home is in seeing it as a playground rather than a puzzle.

it needs, layering patterns in your home feels like a fun art project rather than a difficult math problem. And above all, decorating is supposed to be fun!

Creating Pattern Mix Stories

The way you mix patterns in your spaces tells a story. So, when you are creating what I refer to as "pattern mix stories" for the rooms in your home, I suggest that you once again reflect on your design vibe words (see chapter 1) because pattern mixing presents one of the best opportunities for you to give your home personality. Let your design vibe words be your guide as you select the patterns you want to use in your spaces.

Suggestions for Mixing Patterns

There is a lot to consider when it comes to mixing patterns, but I believe thinking in terms of rules can be a bit too limiting and repressive. As I have already mentioned, decorating is meant to be fun, and there is something about decorating rules that always feels like the opposite of fun. However, *guidelines* feel helpful and encouraging, especially because I prefer to think of them simply as *suggestions*. They do not have to be followed unless you want to follow them.

Consider the Scale

Simply speaking, scale refers to the size of a print. Large + Medium

+ Small = Success! If only high school algebra were that easy. But seriously, when it comes to mixing patterns, remembering that one simple design equation will set you up for success every time. Start by choosing your large-scale pattern to be your dominant or main print first and go from there. Layer in medium- and small-scale prints as accents. In general, large-scale patterns work best for larger elements in a space, like rugs, curtain panels, or wallpaper. Medium- and small-scale prints are great options for decorative accents like throw pillows and lampshades.

Stick to a Color Scheme

Using patterns within a particular color scheme creates an almost effortless mix. It's a good idea to keep the 60-30-10 rule (mentioned in chapter 2) in mind, as it can help you select the perfect color scheme for the patterns in your space.

QUICK TIP

A simple, foolproof way to create a pattern mix story is to stick to one color. A monotone mix of patterns works well. Select one color and three to four different patterns all in that same color, and you will end up with a winning mix of patterns regardless of scale.

Contrast Styles

There are two general pattern styles: organic and geometric. They contrast each other beautifully and generally go together like peanut butter and jelly.

- Organic patterns can be real or a bit abstract. They have a lot of movement to them, making it difficult to perceive where the pattern repeats itself. This style includes floral patterns or nature-inspired prints, and anything with a scrolling, swirling, or curving movement.

- Geometric patterns are those that have clean, clear lines. The most commonly used geometric patterns include stripes, polka dots, and plaids.

Think of Leopard Print (or Any Animal Print) as a Neutral

When style icon Jenna Lyons declared leopard print a neutral it was the statement heard round the fashion world. And it is as true for interiors as it is for fashion. There is just something about leopard print, or really any animal print, that seems to work with every color or pattern story and with every design style. It always adds an exciting, unexpected element to a space.

When in Doubt, Add a Black-and-White Geometric Print

You can almost never go wrong with adding a black-and-white geometric print to your pattern mix, no matter what your design vibe is. If you feel uncertain about mixing patterns, add in a black-and-white stripe. A stripe in a black-and-white colorway, whether large-scale or small, horizontal or vertical, is both versatile and timeless.

What matters *most* is that it is your space— your opinion is the only one that matters.

Trust Your Eye

Honestly, I believe this is *the most* important bit of advice I can offer. In the same way that you know exactly how spicy you like your chili, you instinctively know when a mix of patterns looks good (or bad) to you. Trust your instincts. Maybe you prefer having just one bold pattern in a space filled with solids everywhere else. Or maybe you like pops of medium- and small-scale patterns sprinkled around a room as opposed to a room with a dominant pattern or a very pattern-heavy look. Maybe the "rule" is mixing large-, medium-, and small-scale patterns, but you like the tension created between two large-scale prints paired together in your space. Perhaps you like a small throw pillow outfitted in a large-scale floral pattern. What matters *most* is that it is your space—your opinion is the only one that matters. Does that pattern mix story look good to you? If yes, then it's a win!

A Floor-Up Approach

When it comes to introducing patterns to a space or decorating in general, I personally subscribe to a floor-up approach. I believe starting with a room's foundation is the perfect place to begin, so I typically select a rug first before bringing anything else into a space.

An area rug can be the perfect springboard for creating a pattern mix story in a room. It can be the dominant pattern or just a textural backdrop in the design of a space, but either way, nothing pulls a room together quite like a rug does.

A floor-up approach to creating a pattern story also works well in spaces where you may not use or need an area rug. In bathrooms or laundry rooms, for example, you may forgo an area rug. However, if you are renovating or building, your floor tile can be the perfect first pattern to select for the space. Once your tile pattern is selected, you can build your pattern mix story from there.

QUICK TIP

Because it is easier to select a paint color to coordinate with a rug than it is to find a rug to coordinate with a paint color, I find that it is almost always best to choose a rug before selecting a paint color for your walls. This is why I like to use a rug as my inspiration piece for creating a whole home color palette.

Coordinating Rugs

A floor-up approach can feel a little tricky in an open-concept floor plan or in spaces where multiple rugs are within view of one another because you must consider how the rugs will coordinate. Area rugs are especially vital in open-concept floor plans, as they help to visually break up the space in the absence of walls. The good news is there is always more than one right answer because once again there are no rules. It all comes down to what looks good to your eye.

Here a few suggestions to help spark your creativity.

Try Mixing In a Natural Fiber Rug or a Cowhide

If you are having trouble finding a rug to coordinate with a patterned rug, try pairing it with either a natural fiber like a jute or sisal, or you can pair it with a cowhide. This is a foolproof, classic combination. Cowhides and faux cowhides are like leopard prints; they are neutrals, so they work well with everything. The bonus is natural fiber rugs are usually offered in an affordable price range, and they bring in a versatile, neutral texture that will never go out of style. Natural fiber rugs and cowhides both pair beautifully with patterned rugs.

Stick to One Color Family

Want to mix multiple patterned rugs? Sticking to one color family is a surefire trick. Different styles, textures, and patterns in rugs will all coordinate beautifully if they are all in the same family of colors. Whether you choose a medley of blues, greens, or reds, sticking to one color family creates a cohesive look among a mix of patterns.

Go for a Black-and-White Geometric

When in doubt, remember you can always bring in a black-and-white geometric print. Whether you have a large-, medium-, or small-scale patterned rug, a black-and-white geometric rug will coordinate perfectly. It works every time, and it creates a wonderfully interesting mix. I have used this trick a few times in my home.

Selecting the Perfect Rug Size for Your Space

The color, texture, and pattern of a rug can pull a room together, but obviously the size should also be taken into consideration. In general, I typically advocate for going with the largest rug that will fit into a space, making sure not to cover any floor vents and allowing

For Bedrooms:
You will want to allow for about 30 inches or so on each side of the bed. After that, the size can vary depending on how much of the floor you want to see in the room.

For Living Rooms:
At least the front two legs of all major furniture pieces in the space should fit on the area rug.

For Dining Rooms:
You will want to add about 24 to 30 inches to each side of the table, allowing for the chairs to remain on the rug when they are pulled away from the table.

for at least four inches to remain between the edge of the rug and the walls to keep the rug from looking cramped.

Where to Try a Bold Pattern

If you are feeling ready to step outside your design comfort zone and you want to introduce a bold pattern into a space but you are not quite sure where to start, I completely understand. Maybe you have your eye on some gorgeous wallpaper, but you just don't know if you want to commit to patterned walls in your bedroom. Or perhaps you have pinned a lot of images of living rooms with patterned sofas on Pinterest, but you don't feel that you can justify the expense for something about which you are not completely certain. Design risks often pay off, but it can be hard to take them because of the investment involved. Here are some pattern ice breakers, if you will—some ideas for easing outside your comfort zone in a slightly less risky way.

Go for a Boldly Patterned Rug

Rugs are not only both the perfect place to start designing a room and a wonderful way to build a pattern story in a space, but they are also the perfect place to go for a bold pattern. Going with a boldly patterned rug or allowing the area rug to be the dominant pattern in a room can feel a little less intimidating since much of the pattern will be covered by furniture. The bonus to using a boldly patterned, *colorful* rug is that it can be the perfect springboard for both the pattern *and* color story in a space. Rugs are also fairly easy to source secondhand, allowing you to purchase something of exceptional quality at a lower cost.

Be Daring in the Pass-Through Spaces

If you are looking to play with a bold pattern in a slightly less intimidating space, look no further than the hallways in your home or consider adding some drama to your powder or laundry room. Those are spaces that no one really "lives" in, even if it does sometimes feel like you spend more time in your laundry room than any other room in your home. What I call the pass-through spaces in a home are the perfect places to go for something a bit daring. A boldly patterned wallpaper in these spaces can be easier to digest because they are not walls that you look at all day, so they feel less risky. And the bonus is the pass-through spaces usually involve less square footage, so they are less of an expense to cover.

Bring In a Statement Chair

A statement chair can also be a fun, low-commitment way to play with an eye-catching pattern in living rooms, dining spaces, and

bedrooms. An upholstered patterned chair can be like an exclamation point in a space. Less expensive than a sofa and taking up a relatively small percentage of the visual space in a room, an upholstered chair is a wonderful place to venture outside of your comfort zone regarding pattern. Keep in mind you do not have to cover an entire chair with the same pattern or material. I had the swivel chair in my living room upholstered with a bold black-and-ivory pattern on the front and a solid black leather on the back. It's a bit of a "party in the front, business in the back" situation, and I love this design mullet of a chair. The solid back of the chair balances the bold pattern on the front, keeping the chair from overwhelming the room.

QUICK TIP

Dining chair slipcovers are a great noncommittal, budget-friendly way to play with pattern in a dining room. And the bonus is they offer family-friendly washability.

The Role of Solids

In the same way that too much red pepper can make a pot of chili almost inedible, a pattern-heavy space can feel overstimulating and overwhelming. This, of course, is all based on personal preference. What is too much pattern for one person may not be enough for another. But keep in mind—no matter how much pattern you prefer or how many different prints you like to layer in a space, every room does need at least a few solids in the mix. Pairing prints with solids adds variety, dimension, and interest in a room. But while solids give the eye a much-needed place to rest, they need not be boring. Solids provide the perfect opportunity to layer in some texture.

The Power of Texture

Texture refers to the feel and appearance of a material or surface. It appeals to our sense of touch. And while oftentimes texture is viewed as a solid in design, depending on the particular material it can actually be more of a subtle pattern. Yet because it adds an almost imperceptible pattern to a space, it is much easier to play with and mix in to a pattern story. I believe that where pattern is the spice in a space, texture is the salt. You do not always realize just how important texture is unless it is missing, and a room feels dull and bland.

Texture is essential, especially in a room outfitted with neutral colors, as it keeps spaces from feeling flat or one-dimensional. It may not be as visually loud or eye-catching as a pattern can be in a space, but it absolutely adds both depth and dimension. Layering in a variety of textures creates visual interest and adds warmth. Texture also greatly adds to the vibe of a room.

The rough, coarser textures of jute rugs and reclaimed wood bring in a warm, rustic vibe. Woven furniture like wicker, rattan, and cane adds a classic, casual feel to a space. The smooth, glossy surfaces of brass, chrome, and glass reflect light and bring in a sleek, sophisticated vibe. Regarding soft furnishings, velvet always feels luxurious, while linen brings in a light, airy vibe. And anything upholstered in a bouclé adds a welcoming, cozy element to a space.

Velvet curtain panels are a go-to for me in bedrooms, as they add a lavish, cozy vibe while bringing in a soft, luxe layer of texture. I even added velvet curtain panels to our main bathroom as a way of connecting the bedroom to the bathroom and introducing a healthy dose of texture to a mostly sleek space.

QUICK TIP

Using a patterned fabric as a decorative trim on solid curtain panels is a simple, affordable way to play with pattern in a smaller dose. In addition, this gives solid curtains a custom look.

My Favorite Texture: Grasscloth!

Furnishings are not the only avenue for bringing texture into a room. One of my favorite ways to use texture in my home is through grasscloth on both walls and ceilings. I just love the organic vibe that grasscloth brings to a space, and I have used it in various applications throughout my home.

My vaulted bedroom ceiling is covered in a beautiful tight-weave black grasscloth that brings in a lovely subtle texture to the room while also making the space appear larger. The hallway that leads from the main bedroom to the living room is also covered in grasscloth, this one with a bit more texture and color with a much larger weave than the grasscloth on the bedroom ceiling. To create house flow, I had that same grasscloth added to the walls in the guest bath.

I also lined the back of my living room bookshelves with leftover grasscloth from the main bedroom ceiling project. In my dining room, I used a patterned striped grasscloth on the walls. And when an unfortunate ceiling leak damaged the black grasscloth on the dining room ceiling, I painted over it with a soft shade of blue (to match my kitchen island) because I just could not bring myself to say goodbye to the lovely texture it brought to the space.

In short, grasscloth can be a great option for the pattern-shy decorator who wants to play with wallpaper without committing to a bold pattern. It comes in a variety of colors and styles, and is a more subtle option for pattern that adds beautiful texture to a space and is anything but boring. Though there are patterned grasscloth

QUICK TIP

Color is not the only avenue you can use to create design flow in a home. Repeating patterns work to tie spaces together in the same way as repeating colors.

QUICK TIP

If you ever decide to paint over grasscloth wallpaper, be sure to use a primer for an even paint application that will require fewer coats of paint.

options as well, like the striped grasscloth I hung in my dining room, in general and from a DIY perspective, a traditional non-printed grasscloth is often easier to hang than patterned wallpaper because you do not have to align a print as you install it.

Ideas for Playing with Patterned Wallpaper in Small Doses

Grasscloth is great, but nothing makes more of a design statement in a space than a patterned wallpaper. Although if you are new to playing with patterned wallpaper, I understand that for many reasons you may want to first dip your toe in the shallow end of the pool instead of jumping off the diving board. There is no doubt that patterned wallpaper is both a design commitment and a financial investment. However, there are plenty of ways to use patterned paper in smaller, lower-commitment, budget-friendly doses. Here are a few ideas to get you started:

Only Wallpaper the Top or Bottom Half of a Room

There is no rule that says you must cover the whole wall with your chosen wallpaper. And if there was, we do not have to follow any rules we do not wish to follow. Adding a chair rail and breaking up the pattern by painting half of the wall can give the eye a place to rest, especially in a space where there are two bold patterns. I paired a black-and-white checkerboard tile floor with a red, floral-patterned wallpaper in my laundry room. And to keep these two statement-making patterns from overwhelming the small space, I painted the bottom half of the wall black. Not only does the solid black on the bottom half of

the wall break up the patterns, but it was a much less expensive way to add wallpaper to my laundry room.

Paper the Back of Bookshelves

I have done this with grasscloth wallpaper in two of our homes, and each time I have loved the result. It's a very straightforward, beginner-friendly DIY project that can easily be tackled in a weekend. And while I will always love the texture that grasscloth brings to a space, I think opting for a printed wallpaper would be a fun way to bring in a splash of pattern.

Dress up a Closet

Closets are often overlooked from a design perspective because they are utilitarian spaces that guests rarely (if ever) see. But *you* see your closets every day, so why not make those spaces special just for your own enjoyment? I added leftover wallpaper from my laundry room project to the back of my linen closet, and it *almost* makes me excited when I have to fold and put away towels. Plus, it absolutely motivates me to keep this closet organized.

QUICK TIP

While not all peel-and-stick wallpapers are made the same, there are some excellent quality options available. For closet projects, peel-and-stick wallpapers are both budget-friendly and easy to DIY. As a bonus, they are renter-friendly as well. The floral wallpaper in my laundry room and linen closet is peel-and-stick wallpaper from Spoonflower.

Add It to a Frame

If you want to bring wallpaper into a space without applying it to your walls, try framing wallpaper panels. This is a great option from a design commitment standpoint since it allows for extremely easy and quick removal if or when you are ready for a change (thus it is also a wonderful option for renters). It is a less-expensive way to play with wallpaper since it requires much less square footage.

In addition to framing panels, wallpaper makes a great backdrop for framing art prints. You can use it to cover a photo mat, or you can layer a print or photo directly on top of the wallpaper inside your frame. This creates such an interesting, unique look and is a fantastic way to make use of leftover wallpaper from larger projects. It can also be a wonderful way to use your collection of wallpaper samples.

Add Wallpaper to a Piece of Furniture

Another way to bring wallpaper into a space, besides adding it to walls, is through furniture. This simple, budget-friendly idea not only allows you to play with a patterned paper you love, but it also creates a completely unique piece of furniture. Whether you line the back of an old china cabinet, cover the top of a coffee table, desk, or nightstand, or add it to dresser drawer fronts, using wallpaper on furniture is an interesting, unexpected way to breathe new life into a tired piece of furniture. And these one-of-a-kind pieces add so much personality to a space.

Wallpapered Dresser Drawer Fronts

Adding wallpaper to the fronts of dresser drawers is a beginner-friendly DIY project that can easily be completed in about an hour. You can use traditional, non-pasted wallpaper, pre-pasted, or an adhesive-backed peel-and-stick option for this project.

I used leftover striped grasscloth wallpaper from my dining room project to cover the drawer fronts of a dresser I use as a sideboard in my living room. Leftover wallpaper always calls out to me, begging me to put it to use! I love how this brings the pattern from the dining room walls over to the other side of my open-concept living space.

SUPPLIES NEEDED

–Cleaning supplies
–Pencil
–Measuring tape
–Fine-grit sandpaper
–Paintbrush
–Wallpaper primer (needed only if wallpapering unpainted furniture)
–Wallpaper paste (not needed if you are using a pre-pasted or peel-and-stick wallpaper)
–Wallpaper smoothing tool
–Scissors
–Razor blade

STEP-BY-STEP PROCESS

Step 1: Start with a thorough cleaning and remove any furniture hardware.

Step 2: Measure your drawer fronts. Mark and cut your wallpaper, allowing for an extra quarter of an inch or so on all sides.

NOTE

Traditional, non-pasted wallpaper requires the use of wallpaper paste for installation. Whereas pre-pasted wallpaper already has a paste on the back that is activated with water and can be applied to the wall or other surface once the paste becomes sticky.

QUICK TIP

For any and all DIY wallpaper projects, it is always better to err on the too-large side. Cut panels that are a bit larger than your measurement can easily be trimmed to fit, whereas panels that are even just a tad too short or small often end up being unusable for your project.

Step 3: If you are using a peel-and-stick wallpaper, you can skip over to Step 6. Otherwise, use fine-grit sandpaper to lightly sand the drawer fronts and wipe away dust to prepare the surface.

Step 4: If you are wallpapering a painted piece of furniture, you can skip this step, as the paint acts as a primer. However, if you are adding wallpaper to unpainted furniture, you will want to apply a thin layer of wallpaper primer. Allow the primer to dry completely before moving on to the next step.

QUICK TIP

Wallpaper primer not only allows for better overall adhesion, but it also makes removal much easier. This is true for all wallpaper installations, not just furniture projects.

Step 5: If you are using pre-pasted wallpaper, you will not need to use wallpaper paste. Instead, you will activate the paste on the back of the paper. For traditional, non-pasted wallpaper, use a paintbrush to add a thin layer of wallpaper paste to each drawer front, one at a time, then cover the drawer with your chosen paper. Repeat with each drawer.

Step 6: Place your precut wallpaper panel on the drawer front and use the smoothing tool to work out any air bubbles. Carefully trim the edges with a razor blade.

Step 7: Reinstall the furniture hardware and marvel at your beautiful "new" one-of-a-kind dresser.

QUICK TIP

When working with wallpaper, it is always advisable to use a brand-new razor blade. If you do not already own a wallpaper smoothing tool, a silicone spatula or even a credit card will do the trick for a small wallpaper project like this.

I like an empty wall because I can imagine what I like on it.

GEORGIA O'KEEFE

CHAPTER FOUR

Letting Your Walls Tell Your Story

My favorite part of moving into a new home? Hands down, it is the empty walls! While packing and unpacking and pretty much everything else that goes into moving is absolutely exhausting, a house full of blank walls is nothing but exciting to me! The possibilities feel endless, as I see the walls in a house as blank canvases—or better yet, *blank pages*. The walls of your home provide the perfect opportunity for you to tell your unique story.

What you choose to hang on your walls says so much about you, and nothing gives a home more of a distinctive personality than wall decor. What we choose to adorn our walls with is what truly makes a house feel like a home. The walls of our homes give us the chance to celebrate what we love through paintings, prints, photographs, and so much more.

What we hang on our walls is for nothing more than decoration. After all, wall decor is not meant to serve a function, although it absolutely has a purpose. I mean sure, a clock and a mirror provide function in addition to form. But for the most part, the sole purpose of wall decor is to allow us to express ourselves. Function is almost entirely removed from the equation, and there is something about the pureness of decorating solely for form that feels so fun and freeing!

I see the walls in a house as blank canvases—or better yet, *blank pages*.

From years of messages from readers of my online community, I know that blank walls can feel challenging. While blank canvases or blank pages feel exciting and inspiring for some, others see them as a major design hurdle. When it comes to the walls in a home, it can take time to collect pieces and figure out exactly how you want to hang them. While I find blank walls inspiring, I am never in a rush to fill them. And in many cases, I have lived with empty walls for months, even years in some rooms, because I would rather stare at blank walls and wait for inspiration to strike than force the process. I hope learning this takes some of the pressure off for you before we dive into this chapter. In my opinion, good stories take time to write, and blank walls take time to fill.

Perhaps you need some fresh ideas to spark your creativity, or maybe you could use some helpful advice to motivate you to finally hang that gallery wall you have been procrastinating on for far too long. Whatever aspect of wall decor has been a hurdle for you, I hope this chapter leaves you feeling inspired, confident, and ready to put some nail holes in your walls. I promise, when your walls are filled with pieces you cherish, those that reflect your personality and tell your unique story, you will find yourself falling more in love with your home.

Selecting What to Hang

I see art as the design element that gives a home a soul. Art adds ambiance and so much personality to a space! And so, because it is an expression of who we are, one might think selecting it would be simple and easy, a second-nature design choice. But you know how some days you really struggle to put an outfit together, and other days you can pick out exactly what you want to wear in less than five minutes? Well, dressing your walls can be a lot like that too. In fact, many people feel that selecting *what* to hang on their walls is the most difficult part of decorating. If this resonates and you struggle with selecting art for your home, I have two tips that I hope will be helpful.

Tip Number 1: Choose Art That Feels Personal

First, go for something that feels personal. Why? Because you can never go wrong with selecting art for your home that makes you feel something or brings back special memories.

Frame Keepsakes and Mementos

Look beyond your typical prints and paintings. Selecting art for your walls does not have to be complicated and it need not be expensive for it to be both beautiful and meaningful. Framing keepsakes and mementos not only feels personal but can also be a budget-friendly way to add art to your walls. Why not frame your grandmother's silk scarves or the playbills from all your favorite Broadway shows? *Anything* can be art, and *you* are the art curator of your home.

The first piece of wall art I hung in our very first home was a framed fortune cookie message that my husband used to propose to me. A little Chinese restaurant called Peking Dragon in Dana Point, California, hosted our first date, many dates after that, our engagement, and our rehearsal dinner. This framed fortune holds so much meaning and so many great memories that it has rightfully hung in every house we have called home over the past twenty-four years.

My guess is you have some great keepsakes and mementos in storage bins just waiting for their chance to shine. It is time to climb those attic stairs or sift through that basement closet so you can frame those special treasures. Here are some things I love the idea of framing:

- Wedding invitations
- Birth announcements (This lovely idea for a nursery can later be added to a family photo gallery wall.)
- Concert tickets (Oh, how I wish I had held onto my first concert ticket to see Prince!)
- Postcards (My mom framed a postcard my grandmother sent from the ship that brought her from Japan to the United States, and every time I see it I'm in awe of my grandmother's incredible strength.)
- Love letters
- Sheet music
- Recipe cards
- Puzzles (My grandfather loved working on crossword puzzles, and he had the best handwriting! I know many families who have traditions around working a puzzle whether during vacations or holidays, and I love the idea of framing a completed puzzle and having every member of the family sign their name on it along with the year it was completed.)

- Outgrown children's clothes (Bathing suits and swim trunks are a fun idea for a bathroom.)
- Children's art (Without question, some of my favorite pieces of art I have displayed in our home are those made by my children. And the older they get, the more I cherish these precious pieces.)

For Mother's Day one year, my daughter—who was in fourth grade at the time—made me a card in which she put on lipstick and gave me a bunch of kisses on the paper. I loved it so much that I framed it almost immediately. As I write this book, she is a senior in high school just months away from graduating, and this framed card brings back so many precious memories.

If you are struggling to source art for your home, take a look at what you already have. Frame and hang the things that make you smile.

QUICK TIP

There are quite a few different phone apps available, some free and some that charge a nominal fee, that make creating custom art prints from photos extremely easy and affordable. Doing a quick search in your app store will allow you to check out the available options. Print quality in larger sizes may not be as great compared to what you might find going through an artist on Etsy or an online art store like Minted, but for smaller print sizes, this could be a great, much more affordable option for getting the look of custom artwork that is created from a special photo.

Custom Art

While nothing is quite as special as framed keepsakes or mementos, custom art can be just as personal and meaningful. And contrary to what the word *custom* might lead you to believe, there are a lot of affordable ways to bring custom art into your home. In addition, sourcing artists who offer custom pieces is easier than it has ever been thanks to sites like Etsy and social media where it is easy for shoppers to find and connect with independent artists.

Even Minted, a large, well-known online art store, offers custom artwork at a wide variety

of price points along with great framing options. From custom silhouettes and watercolor venue prints to custom pet and house portraits, their bespoke options offer something for every occasion, budget, and style.

It might be because we have moved quite a few times and have called so many houses home over the years, but I love custom house portraits. To me they are the art version of a time capsule, and they become even more special when you move, as they represent where you have been and add immediate history to the walls of your new home. I also like the idea of having them made of childhood homes.

A few years ago, after connecting with an artist I discovered on Instagram, I had simple, classic, black-and-white house portraits made of our six previous homes.

And they are easily among my most treasured pieces of art, just second to those made by my children. Each house portrait brings back so many fond memories. Hanging all six of these pieces together in the hallway off our entry foyer tells the story of our moving adventures so perfectly:

1. The very first house we ever called home
2. The grey stone house with the double-sided fireplace I loved
3. The home in Virginia where we welcomed both of our babies

4. The 1954 Cape Cod–style house we fell in love with in Pittsburgh
5. The house that inspired me to start my blog, *Our Fifth House*, in Lexington, Kentucky
6. The house that brought us to South Carolina

No other wall in our current home tells our story quite like this one. While I have yet to have a custom portrait made of our current home, as the artist who made all our other portraits no longer does them, I plan to have one made by a different artist someday.

Created by You

Maybe you're thinking about skipping over this section because you do not see yourself as an artist. But trust me, there is a creator in all of us. I genuinely believe that. I also believe that you do not have to be an artist to create artwork that you will feel proud to hang on the walls of your home. Ask me how I know.

While keepsakes, mementos, and custom pieces are wonderful ways to fill the walls of your home with meaningful art, what could be more personal than art you make yourself? I am certainly not an artist, and I have taken a total of zero art classes (unless you count elementary school). To be fully transparent, my fifth-grade teacher actually told me I lacked creativity because of a less-than-great 3D model I made of the state of Wyoming. And while my project likely deserved the C it was given, she was wrong about me. I am glad I refused to let her critique define me. There is a creative in all of us because we were made in the image of a Creator. We just need to feel inspired.

it was the best of times, the worst of crimes

Making a house feel like a home fills my inspiration cup to over-flowing! While I do not have the schooling or the talent of a professional artist, I did not let that stop me from creating art for my home. Maybe these simple ideas will inspire your own creativity.

Painted Quote over a Print

I found a framed giclée print on canvas (a reproduction of *The End of Dinner*, by Jules-Alexandre Grün) at Goodwill that was just slightly warped. I had initially planned to keep the frame and discard the damaged art.

However, once I had this piece in my home, I realized the colors were perfect for my powder room. I decided to have a little fun in an effort to distract the eye from the fact that the printed canvas was a little warped. Using white acrylic paint and a brush, I freehand painted a favorite song lyric over the print. I am a Swiftie, and "Getaway Car" is one of my favorite songs. The juxtaposition of the painted words against this post-impressionist dinner scene is unexpected and fun. Does this count as art I made myself? Maybe not *exactly*. But I gave it my own spin, so I am including it here. The moral of this story is not to take decorating so seriously. Take some risks! And shop second-hand. That makes experimenting feel a lot less scary.

Abstract Paper Collage

The bonus to making your own art is that it is a very affordable way to add large-scale pieces to your walls. A few years ago, I decided to try my hand at making a large abstract paper collage to hang over the sofa in my husband's office that doubles as our guest bedroom. I love abstract art, especially in spaces with traditional moldings. Having just come across a sale on canvases at a local craft supply store, I felt like I didn't have much to lose. Truth be told, I figured I could just use whatever I made as a place holder until I found something else. But I fell in love with my simple creation.

By combining acrylic paint with pieces of paper I cut into squares and rectangles and laying them in a weaved pattern, I created an abstract collage that feels modern and interesting. It adds texture, dimension, and movement to the room.

Fabric Vase Collage

Wanting to bring the wallpaper pattern in my laundry room all the way around the room in an unconventional way, I opted to use the same pattern in velvet fabric to create a collage. This one was inspired by this William Morris floral print. I made a vase of flowers by carefully cutting out the flowers in the pattern. To create the illusion of a frame, I painted a scalloped border.

Hand-Painted Wall Mural

Admittedly, this is not a simple or easy project, but I have chosen to include it here as proof that you need not be an artist to paint a mural in your home. Three generations of women brought the mural in my daughter's bedroom to life: my daughter, my mom, and me. Inspired by the mural in the teenage girl's bedroom in the Netflix series *To All the Boys I've Loved Before*, my daughter requested that I create a similar look. And I am not going to lie, my initial reaction was to show her a few different *wallpapers*. Because, as I have already mentioned, I am *not* an artist. And this felt like a huge undertaking. She, however, was firmly against wallpaper and really wanted something hand-painted. With wisdom beyond her

QUICK TIP

The art section at Goodwill is a treasure trove! Do not let a great frame pass you by simply because the artwork is not your style. The frame alone is likely worth the price.

young years, she said, "If it doesn't work out, you can always paint over it." So, I figured I needed to show her what it looks like to step outside your comfort zone. We worked on this wall mural together back in 2020 at the very beginning of the pandemic. Two years later, my mom—who actually *is* an artist—was able to visit us from Southern California. She added the final touches, bringing in some birds and butterflies to this whimsical garden scene. Without question, I will never paint over this mural that holds so many precious memories and has become so special to all three of us.

Tip Number 2: It Does Not Have to Be That Deep

My second suggestion regarding art selections for your home might sound contradictory to my first suggestion. However, while choosing art that feels meaningful or reflects your personal history is wonderful, selecting art for your home does not have to be that deep. You are totally allowed to choose art simply because you love it. That you love it is what makes it personal. It really can be that simple. And it is worth repeating, but it absolutely does not have to be expensive for it to be beautiful. If you are struggling to select art for a particular space, circle back to your design vibe words and let them be your guide. Wall art is the cherry on top of a room design, so have some fun with your selections!

Framing Ideas

If the art you have selected does not quite fit within the typical pre-made framing sizes, obviously, you can go the custom framing route or have a custom mat made to fit your piece within a store-bought frame. Conversely, you could skip the custom route altogether and try one of these options.

Layer It over a Piece of Wallpaper

The bonus of collecting wallpaper samples is that I always have a bunch of options on hand. So, I have used this trick of a wallpaper background a few times in my home when framing both the hand-made cards my mom sends me for my birthday and my children's artwork. This is an easy trick that gives smaller pieces of art a bit more presence while also helping you to avoid the cost of custom framing. And if you are a wallpaper sample collector like I am, you can switch out the wallpaper easily whenever you are ready for a change.

Frame a Frame

Speaking of collecting, I've already mentioned that I am a big fan of the frame and art department at Goodwill. Vintage frames are some of my favorite items to hunt for when I am secondhand shopping. I often find open-back frames that are missing the glass and backing. And I could, of course, take them to a custom frame shop. However, I like to instead use them to frame a frame.

This easy framing idea helps me avoid the cost of custom framing, while also creating an interesting, unique art statement. Pairing an ornate vintage frame with a modern frame is my favorite combination, but you could use any style frame you like to create this look. This is another great trick to pull out when you want to make a smaller piece of art appear larger.

Wall art
is the
cherry on top
of a
room design.

When in Doubt, Go for a Mirror

If you are having a tough time deciding what to hang in a space, a mirror is often a good option. You will just want to be mindful of what the mirror is reflecting. Will it reflect a ceiling fan? In that case, a mirror might not be your best choice. However, if the mirror reflects a gorgeous chandelier or a piece of art from across the room, it would be a wonderful option.

Mirrors increase natural light, so they can be especially useful in dark, dimly lit spaces. Positioning a mirror across from a window will reflect light back into a room while creating the illusion of more space.

The Art of Arranging Art in a Room

As you already know, I am not a huge fan of design rules, but guidelines or helpful suggestions can be, well, helpful. And with typical rooms having four walls, arranging art can be as much of a challenge as selecting art. I think the trick to successfully arranging art in a room is to hang something different on every wall. Rather than hanging one large piece of art on every single wall, think about creating a collection of art in your space by mixing things up and choosing one of the following options for each wall in your room:

- One single piece—either a small, medium, or large piece of art (depending on the size of your wall)
- Stacked pieces of art
- Art arranged in a grid pattern
- Mirror
- Gallery wall

Hanging Art with Confidence

Interior designers tend to share a lot of rules with specific measurements regarding how to hang art correctly. And while it can be helpful to learn that art should be hung about 57 inches from the floor, there are exceptions to every rule. Things such as ceiling height as well as the size of the art should be taken into consideration. So rather than sharing specific measurements, here are a few tips I think will be easier to remember and will hopefully boost your art-hanging confidence:

- Most importantly, hang your art so the middle of the piece is at eye level. Unless you are taller than the average person, this will work every time. If you are second-guessing yourself, keep in mind that you are *always* better off hanging art too low than too high.
- Allow your art to cover as much of the wall as possible. Practically stated, hang large art or art collections on large walls and small art on small walls. Basically, you do not want your art to get lost on your wall and look too small.
- Treat collections or groups of art as one large piece with the centerpiece hung at eye level.
- Art hung above furniture—whether a sofa, bed, or console table—should feel related to the furniture. The bottom of your art should not be too high from the top of your piece of furniture.

Don't be afraid to break the rules. Sometimes a small piece of art hung on a large wall can make a bold statement.

How to Start a Gallery Wall

Perhaps because I am a bit of an art hoarder–I mean *collector*–in my opinion a gallery wall is always a good idea! Although, I know that because there are so many ways to create a gallery wall, getting started can sometimes feel a little intimidating. Even just the physical hanging of your collection of frames can be its own special kind of headache, which we will tackle together in just a bit. Curating a collection of pieces you want to hang together should feel fun, not stressful. The curating or collecting part of creating a gallery wall is the best part!

Start by Deciding What Story You Want to Tell

Because I view the walls of my home as blank pages, I always like to start a gallery wall by thinking about the story I want it to tell. Focusing on the story helps me to curate the paintings, prints, and photographs I want to display. This storytelling method of curating yields a collection of pieces that feels incredibly meaningful and personal.

There are so many different stories you can tell with a gallery wall in your home, from highlighting your interests to sharing your family history. Do you enjoy traveling? A wall of vacation prints, trip souvenirs, and destinations you hope to visit someday tells a compelling story, reminds you of the beautiful places you have visited, and inspires you to keep dreaming about your next trip.

I know you have a lot of stories you can tell about your life, your interests, and your dreams. Let those stories guide you when you are curating pieces for a gallery wall.

Let the Color Palette of the Room Inspire You

Once you have a story in mind, pull inspiration from the color palette of the room as you start collecting pieces for your gallery wall.

A Simple Guide to Hanging a Gallery Wall the "Right" Way

So, you have curated all the pieces you want to hang on your gallery wall. Now what? The hanging part can be a little tricky, huh? I mean, it's not rocket science, and yet installing a gallery wall can feel quite daunting. Your collection of frames is staring you down as it is just waiting to be hung on your wall, and maybe you are not quite sure where to start and you are feeling nervous about getting it wrong. So you let the frames sit on the floor leaning against the wall collecting dust as you say to yourself that someday you will get around to hanging your collection.

Let me give you a little encouragement, because here is the thing: It's not your collection of frames or your big, empty wall that is holding you back. It's your mindset. So let me take the pressure off by sharing this truth: You cannot get a gallery wall wrong. There is no one right way. Relax. You've got this! Here are a few suggestions to get you started.

QUICK TIP

Take architectural photos when you are traveling. I started doing this years ago. Not because I am a great photographer but because even a mediocre picture of a beautiful door in Positano looks incredible in a frame. Sure, vacation photos featuring you and your family are great, but photos of architectural details, landscapes, or whatever catches your eye make for great "free" souvenirs and wonderful framed art for your home.

Play with the Arrangement on the Floor

I like to start the hanging process by playing with my collection of frames on the floor until I land on an arrangement I really like. This is where I focus on balancing color, making sure to keep the color moving throughout the gallery wall.

Make Sure Your Collection Has a Leader

Before you start hanging, choose a leader for your collection. Some decorators refer to this piece as an anchor, but what you call this piece is inconsequential. The takeaway is that every great gallery wall has at least one large-scale piece that grounds, anchors, or leads the rest of the collection. When you have a collection of pieces that are all the same size or that are all on the smaller side, the collection can feel a little chaotic. Having at least one strong, large piece in the mix holds all the smaller pieces together. You can have more than one large piece but, at the very least, one helps to give the collection an anchor point. It also gives you the perfect place to start when you begin to hang.

Start Off-Center

Start by hanging your leader or anchor piece first. But just because she is your fearless leader does not mean she should be the center-piece of the collection. Your best bet is to hang her off-center. I like to think that the goal with a gallery wall is to create one cohesive story from multiple interesting pieces. You do not need your fearless leader to take center stage. Every piece deserves a place to shine.

Vary Sizes and Orientation as You Are Hanging

While including at least one large piece provides an anchor for your collection, smaller pieces are great to fill in gaps and keep things interesting. Mixing up your horizontal, vertical, and even square or round pieces creates both movement and balance.

QUICK TIP

If you are building a gallery wall around a television, as I did in our bedroom, you will likely want your television to be the centerpiece. Then hang your next largest piece off-center and build on from there.

Keep Your Spacing Even-ish

Overthinking the spacing of every single frame will just bog you down and stifle your creativity. After all, perfection and collection are two words that do not really go that well together, in my opinion. It is a waste of precious brain space to fret too much over spacing. You want to pay attention to it but it need not interrupt your creative flow. Try to mimic spacing throughout your gallery wall. For example, if you have some frames hung an inch apart and some hung two or three inches apart, try to use that spacing in various places throughout your gallery wall. Think balance—not perfection. Just try to get the spacing to be even-*ish*.

Perfection and collection are two words that do not really go that well together.

Creating a Family Photo Gallery Wall

For me, a house is just not a home without family photos, which is why a family photo gallery wall is my favorite kind of gallery wall.

Family photos add so much life to a home, and hanging them gallery style makes a beautiful statement. I especially love those that leave room to grow. While matching frames can be great, I prefer the collected look of mismatched frames.

Mix Up the Frames, Both in Size and Style

If you want to continue to add photos to your wall over time, I think it's best to start out with a good mix of frames, this way the newest additions will always blend in with the frames you already have on your wall. Even if you want to use frames in all one color, mixing in assorted styles will create a nice, collected look that you can add on to in the future.

Consider a Color Story

Black-and-white photos are my personal favorite because they make it easy to mix old family photos with new ones. Also, even the worst iPhone photo looks pretty great in black and white. However, if you prefer color photos, you might want to consider a color story and select photos that fit within a certain color palette so that the photos on display will mesh well together.

Shell Art Grid Wall

If the art projects I shared in the "Created by You" section of this chapter felt like too much for you, I promise that making your own art does not get simpler than this shell art project. Seriously, this one is so easy it hardly qualifies as a do-it-yourself project. And the bonus is that it is beyond budget-friendly, as it is virtually free! While I would not define my interior vibe as coastal, having grown up in Southern California and now living just a few miles from the beach in South Carolina, I am a shell collector. I have always loved a shell moment in my home decor because of what shells represent for me. They remind me of special memories, and just looking at them fills me with gratitude. You could make just one frame, but since this is such an easy, low-cost project, why not make a bunch, hang them grid-style, and make a large shell art statement in your home?

SUPPLIES NEEDED

–Seashells
–Small, old paintbrush
–E6000 glue

–Black acrylic paint or black cardstock
–White photo mats
–Picture frames

STEP-BY-STEP PROCESS

Step 1: Paint the inside back of each picture frame with black acrylic paint or place a piece of black cardstock inside each frame. (Using black creates a nice high-contrast backdrop for the shells, but you can use any color you want.)

Step 2: Add white photo mats to the frames.

Step 3: Using an old paintbrush, add E6000 glue to the edges of your seashells and glue them to the glass fronts of each frame.

Step 4: Allow the glue to cure for about 24 hours and then hang your shell art frames!

QUICK TIP

E6000 is the best glue for a project like this. It provides a strong bond once completely cured, allows for wiggle room during application, and dries clear. The best part is you will not accidentally glue your fingers together as sometimes happens with superglue.

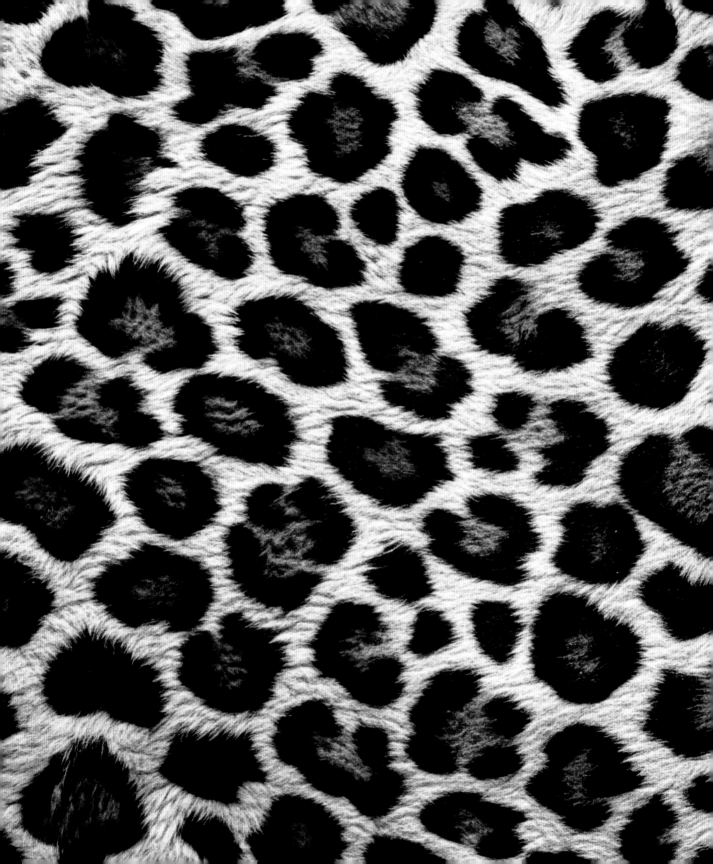

Furniture must
have a personality,
as well as be beautiful.

ROSE TARLOW

CHAPTER FIVE

Curating Furniture That Conveys Your Unique Design Vibe

I love the quote on the previous page from Los Angeles–based interior and furniture designer, Rose Tarlow. Not only because I wholeheartedly agree with this sentiment but even more so because I absolutely, completely, and resoundingly *adore* the idea of carefully curating furniture for our homes through the lens of personality. In my opinion, furniture is the design element that invites you into a room. Where color sets the mood, furniture introduces the attitude.

While no other design element marries function with form quite like furniture, I love the way a personality lens encourages us to view furniture from an emotional place. It inspires us to reflect on how a piece of furniture makes us *feel*. And by now you know, when it comes to creating a home, I am all about homing in on the design *vibe* of a space over the design look. What better way to thoughtfully collect furniture that conveys our unique design vibe than to reflect on the personality that each individual piece brings into our homes. Viewing furniture from a personality perspective means we do not have to be pro interior designers or furniture experts to curate pieces we love!

Without uttering a single word, furniture bosses us around. It tells us where to sit, eat, and sleep. And the way I see it, *how* it tells us what to do is all dependent on personality. The style, material, pattern, texture, and color of the pieces of furniture we choose has a major impact on the overall design vibe of a space. Have you ever thought about your furniture from a personality perspective?

Does your furniture softly whisper, "Hey, come on in and get cozy here"? Or is your furniture a bit sassier, louder, and bolder? Does your sofa give you a high five when you walk into your living room, or does it open its arms for a soft embrace? Is your dining table wellworn and ready for art projects, homework, coloring Easter eggs, and whatever else your family might throw at it, or is it perfectly polished and politely ready to serve a beautiful meal at your next dinner party?

Curating a collection of furniture that conveys your unique design vibe can truly be an art form in and of itself, but it is also a skill that can most definitely be learned and sharpened. Bringing a room together with different pieces may seem a bit intimidating at first, especially so if you're not quite sure where to begin. However, with a few simple guidelines, or rather, helpful suggestions, you will be well on your way to curating an intentionally mixed and

matched collection of furniture that perfectly captures your personal design vibe.

Where to Begin

Before we get to the ins and outs of mixing and matching furniture, we need to do a little design homework. I promise that this small investment of your time will absolutely pay dividends. When it comes to furniture, my guess is if you are reading this book, you are not starting from scratch, even if you have just moved in to your very first place. Depending on the season of life you're currently living in, you might have already collected quite a few pieces of furniture, possibly inherited a few heirlooms, or have been the happy or not-so-happy recipient of a few hand-me-downs. Maybe somewhere along the way you have invested in some important basics like a great sofa or a well-made bed, picked up a few affordable pieces at Ikea or Target, or have found a few treasures at a thrift store or an estate sale. So where do you begin when it comes to curating the perfect mix of furniture that captures your unique design vibe? Start by *editing* what you already have.

A Brutally Honest Furniture Edit

Wardrobe stylists regularly recommend their clients do a clothing edit—and for good reason. It is so important and hugely beneficial to examine what you already have and purge what no longer serves you before you start bringing in anything new. The same is true in your home, especially with furniture!

Before you bring in any new pieces of furniture, I believe it is best to start with a really great edit. Room by room, take an inventory of the furniture you currently have and reflect on the design vibe words you chose for your home back in chapter 1. Examine every single piece of furniture you own and be brutally honest with yourself. Grab your design notebook and a pencil and create a list of the pieces that do not fit your design vibe or that you no longer love. Be sure to jot down your why, noting the specific reasons you have added each piece to your edit list. Trust me, this will come in handy later. Your home is your sanctuary, and it should be filled only with what you love.

QUICK TIP

This is also a great exercise to do before you begin packing for a move! Ask me how I know.

Don't get mad at the messenger, but friends, "this works" is not a good enough reason to keep a piece of furniture off your edit list. What you need to ask yourself are two very important questions:

1. Do I *love* this piece? I don't mean kind of like or feel okay about, but *love*. If not, it needs to go on your edit list.
2. Does it fit at least one of my design vibe words? It may not fit all three of your design vibe words, but it needs to fit at least one.

As you already know, design rules are not my favorite, but this is a design *truth,* and it is one I believe to my core. Simply stated, you absolutely cannot create a space you love around a piece of furniture you hate. It just is not possible. Every piece of furniture in your home should be something you love that also fits your desired design vibe. Although, as we will discuss in the next section, a furniture edit is not solely about purging what no longer serves you. The added benefit of creating a furniture edit list is that it helps you to further hone your desired design vibe.

The Beauty of Creating a Furniture Edit List

Now, listen, I am certainly not saying you need to get rid of every single piece of furniture on your edit list right away or even that every piece of furniture on your edit list needs to be purged at all. Purging furniture is not as simple, easy, or financially practical as purging your wardrobe. After all, furniture is not just about form. You need somewhere to sit and sleep and a place to set down your mug of coffee that eternally needs to be rewarmed. All I am suggesting, or more accurately, *advocating* for, is that you utilize your edit list as a jumping-off point or a springboard.

Creating a furniture edit list is truly less about purging and more about identifying which pieces of furniture you already own that do and do not fit your desired design vibe. What you might not yet realize is your furniture edit list can be the key to unlocking your creativity. Is there anything on your edit list that you might love if you made a few changes? You see, the beauty of starting with your edit list is that these are the pieces you already don't like or at the very least the ones that do not fit your desired design vibe. So, you have added them to your edit list because you are thinking about getting rid of them. Which means that if you experiment with the piece, you have nothing to lose and everything to gain! Think of your furniture edit list as your permission slip to play.

Hunting for Potential on Your Edit List

Creating your furniture edit list is the first step toward curating a collection of furniture you love that conveys your unique design vibe. Step two is all about reexamining every piece of furniture on that list. This is what I like to call "hunting for potential." And in this phase of the process, you refer to the notes you made about each piece of furniture on your edit list (I told you this would come in handy!). Are there any diamonds in the rough here? If you make over, reimagine, or repurpose any of these pieces, would that make you want to cross them off your edit list? Do any of these pieces have staying potential?

From the Edit List to the Staying List

Every piece of furniture on your edit list might not have the potential to move to your staying list. Thankfully, these days, listing pieces on Facebook Marketplace can help to soften the blow of parting ways. But for the contenders on your furniture edit list, here are a few ideas that will hopefully get your creative juices flowing. Sometimes all a piece of furniture needs is a little makeover.

Furniture Makeovers

Paint Can Be Your Best Friend

Furniture purists are often against painting antiques and vintage pieces. However, while I do not believe every old piece of furniture needs to be painted to feel fresh and revitalized, I am most definitely a fan of painted furniture. If a coat of paint allows you to move a piece of furniture off your edit list, I say go for it! This might be controversial, but I honestly believe your grandmother would rather you paint her old dresser and proudly use it in your home than have it collect dust in a storage unit. Furniture was made to be used and appreciated, not stored.

Once upon a time, I had a circa early '80s cherry wood Queen Anne-style dining table and chairs that did not fit my design vibe *at all*. It's kind of a tangled story as to how I ended up with this dining set, but to make a long story short, I paid for the set even though I did not choose it myself. And ~~I just never liked it~~ I always hated it, though I gave it my best effort because I could not afford a replacement.

For years, I tried to decorate around this table and chairs, and I was always dissatisfied with the result. A dining table and chairs are crucial to, you know, a *dining room*, so working around said elephant in the room wasn't exactly easy. No amount of decor could make this table and chairs fit the design vibe I wanted for my home. And then one day, years ago—not long after I started my blog—it dawned on me that I could totally *paint* the table and chairs.

I didn't need to ask anyone for permission! They were my table and chairs, and I could do whatever I wanted! The mere idea that I could paint over "good wood," transforming what was already "nice furniture" solely to fit my personal design vibe felt a little, well, to be honest—scary at first. But once that first coat of primer went on, it was like that "once it hits your lips moment" that Will Ferrell's character has in the movie *Old School*. I felt this incredible surge of empowerment!

That was one of my very first furniture makeovers. And while I eventually sold that table and chairs to a lovely lady on Facebook Marketplace who absolutely loved the makeover and momentarily made me pause and think I should maybe start a furniture rehab business, making over that set allowed me to truly enjoy that table and chairs in my dining room until I was finally able to afford a replacement. And the design lesson I learned from that furniture painting project was invaluable. Don't decorate *around* furniture you hate; instead, do what you can to *change* the furniture you hate.

Paint can absolutely be your best friend. As a color lover, I feel that a pop of color can often be just what a piece needs to give it new life, make it fit my design vibe, and help me love it again. I gave a thrifted side table that was feeling a little too blah and boring for my bedroom design vibe a coat of orange-y red paint, and it was immediately crossed off my furniture edit list. The splash of red was just the bold pop of color my bedroom was craving.

Don't Count Out Stain Stripper

There is no doubt that paint is a wonderful way to freshen up a piece of furniture. However, as I have already mentioned, I do not believe every piece needs a coat of paint. Don't count out the power of using stain stripper to breathe new life into an old piece of furniture. If a piece of furniture looks a bit too rough around the edges or is darker in color than you prefer, stripping the stain down to the raw wood, sanding, and restaining could be just the thing. Check out the DIY Spotlight project at the end of this chapter for inspiration!

New Upholstery Can Be a Game Changer

Sometimes new fabric is all that is needed to help you cross a chair or sofa off your furniture edit list. If the style, shape, quality, and size of the piece works for you, reupholstering is definitely worth considering. Just the other day, I was scrolling Instagram and came

across a reel posted by my friend Ashley (@biggerthanthethreeofus) sharing how she reupholstered her grandmother's old rocking chair. A chair that was once stored away because the original pink fabric wasn't quite the right vibe for Ashley's home was recovered with a vintage rug and is now sitting proudly in the corner of her dining room, adding so much personality to the space. Now the chair combines Ashley's design vibe with her grandmother's, creating a fully unique, meaningful piece.

Many times, even a few smaller upholstery changes, like removing the skirt or adding fringe or a nail head detail, could help to make a piece of furniture better fit your design vibe. A couple of years ago, I stumbled across a great wingback chair for my son's bedroom at my local Goodwill store. The plaid upholstery was in fantastic condition, but the skirt on the chair was not quite the right vibe for his room. So, I removed it and added a nail-head trim, and those two small tweaks made all the difference.

Reimagining and Repurposing

A furniture makeover is often the obvious option when it comes to giving a piece of furniture new life. However, you might also want to consider reimagining a piece or repurposing. Look back at the notes you made on your furniture edit list. Is there a piece on your list that you no longer like for the room it is currently living in, but that you could maybe love again if it were in another room or being used in a slightly different way?

The no-longer-working antique stereo that belonged to my husband's grandparents is a well-loved, meaningful piece of furniture that I struggled with design-wise for years. When we inherited it, the hardware was broken, so first I added new hardware. But because of its size, I had a tough time finding the right place for it in our home. When I stopped seeing it solely as a nonfunctioning antique stereo and embraced all the ways it could be used in our home, inspiration finally hit.

I have since used it as an entry foyer table (in our fifth house), a small hallway console table (in our sixth house), and it now lives in our laundry room. It provides the perfect amount of storage for our laundry soap and things, while the top of the stereo functions well as a folding table. And I love the way it elevates the overall vibe of our laundry.

I am currently using a small vintage book-shelf in my dining room as a barware display cabinet, but this piece could easily be used in a closet as a jewelry organizer or in a kitchen to hold a collection of cookbooks. The brass chest I scored years ago at a consignment store is still a beloved piece of mine, and it has lived many lives in our homes over the years. In the living room of our fifth house I used it as a coffee table, and in our sixth house it was a side table. In our current home it is being used as a nightstand in my son's bedroom. Sometimes all it takes to move a piece of furniture off your edit list is a little reimagining.

QUICK TIP

Adding furniture to utilitarian spaces adds a bit of unexpected charm. Bathrooms, kitchens, laundry rooms, and even closets are great spaces to repurpose pieces of furniture on your edit list. That china cabinet you are no longer crazy about in your dining room might be the perfect statement maker for your main bathroom. Imagine it filled with linens and toiletries! Small side tables, plant stands, and chairs can add an interesting, functional layer to bathrooms as well.

Other Ideas for Updating Furniture

Small changes can have a big impact. Don't underestimate the transformative power of simple projects, like the following ideas.

- **Swap out furniture hardware**.
- **Refresh furniture with Restor-A-Finish**. If you are not already familiar with Restor-A-Finish, this magical liquid is about to become your new obsession for bringing old wood furniture back to life! You can find it at any hardware store, and it is extremely user-friendly—zero DIY skills are required. This easy-to-use formula comes in a wide variety of wood tones and restores tired, old wood by concealing blemishes, watermarks, and minor scratches. All you do is wipe it on with a soft cloth, and let the magic happen. I used it on the vintage piano I scored on Facebook Marketplace a few years ago, and it worked like a charm to refresh the wood finish!
- **Change the legs**. I love the nightstands in my bedroom, but they were a bit too short. To remedy the too-short situation, I swapped out the bun feet that came on the nightstands for longer turned wood feet.
- **Add wallpaper**. (See the DIY Spotlight project in chapter 3.)

QUICK TIP

Typically, a nightstand should be level with the top of the mattress, give or take a few inches.

From an Edit List to a Shopping List

I recommend performing a furniture edit at least once a year because, as I have already mentioned, it sparks creativity. It also helps you to hone your design vibe and keep your spaces feeling fresh. The bonus is it also provides you with a thoughtfully detailed furniture shopping guide. You see, once you have reexamined every line item on your furniture edit list and decided if there are any pieces worth making over or reimagining, you are left with a list of pieces that you want to eventually replace.

And you are now ready to start curating new (or new *old*) pieces of furniture for your home. That's right, you're finally ready to do some shopping! This part of the process could take some time. Rome was not built in a day, and your home does not need to be either. The magic happens along the journey, especially when it comes to mixing and matching furniture!

Curating, A.K.A. *Intentionally* Mixing and Matching Furniture

Mixing and matching furniture with intention is all about purposefully incorporating a variety of styles, textures, patterns, and colors of furniture to create a layered, collected look that feels cohesive and conveys your chosen design vibe. The result of a mixed-and-matched collection, no matter what vibe you are after, is always more visually appealing and truly tells a more interesting story. A variety of different pieces adds depth and character, keeping a space from feeling flat and boring. A mixed-and-matched approach to furnishing a room not only gives a way for you to infuse your spaces with personality but also allows for flexibility with your design choices. It is much easier to swap out individual pieces when you are not committed to any particular style or era. And the bonus is that mixing and matching can be extremely

Rome was not built in a day, and your home does not need to be either.

budget-friendly, as you can slowly add pieces over time rather than purchasing complete sets.

The goal is to create a cohesive space with your various pieces, emphasis on *cohesive*. However, that can be a little challenging. While the best interior designers make it look effortless, a few basic tips can help anyone master the art of mixing and matching to create a space that feels harmonious.

Tip Number 1: Use Color to Unify

A color story can go a long way toward making a room filled with a collection of different furniture pieces feel like they belong together. This is particularly true when upholstered furniture comes into play. Color has this almost magical way of unifying individual pieces to tell one beautifully cohesive story. When it comes to mixing furniture styles and eras together in the same room, color is the key player as it becomes the necessary common thread in the space. I like to imagine that each piece of furniture in a room is like a member of a team with different roles or jobs and every piece is working together to reach the same goal. Adhering to a color story really helps to unify the team.

I think the key to bringing a mixed-and-matched space together with a color story is in utilizing what I like to call a "marrying element." This is the piece that brings the color story together or marries all the colors in the room. It could be a rug or a piece of art, but it could also be in the form of fabric via upholstery, window treatments, or even throw pillows. In our living room, the area rug is the marrying element. In our home library, it is both the rug and a few of the throw pillows that bring all the colors in the room together.

Tip Number 2: Create Balance

Besides color, I believe balance is the key to creating a harmonious look with a curated collection of mixed and matched pieces of furniture. I generally think about creating balance in a space by applying Newton's third law to my design: For every design action there is an equal and opposite design reaction. Essentially, I balance every bold furniture choice with one that is a bit more subdued. In action this looks like pairing a statement chair with a simple glass coffee table or combining a clean round pedestal table with an ornate vintage mirror. It's almost formulaic, and I love the way it creates a balanced, interesting mix of curated furniture in a space.

I generally think about creating balance in a space by applying Newton's third law to my design: For every design action there is an equal and opposite design reaction.

Scale and proportion are also important elements to consider regarding balance when mixing and matching furniture. You would likely not want the size of any single piece to overpower or dominate a room. For example, you wouldn't want to pair a big, overstuffed sofa with a teeny, tiny coffee table. Rather, you would want to balance the size of the sofa with a table that is more substantial.

In addition, a room with several large, overstuffed pieces might feel overpowered, while a room with a lot of small pieces might feel

QUICK TIP

In general, a coffee table should be about two-thirds the length of your sofa.

cluttered. However, a room with a balanced mix of large and small pieces magically feels just right.

The visual weight of furniture is also an important consideration. Darker pieces tend to appear heavier in a room, so you would balance them with lighter pieces. As an example, the black leather chairs in my living room are balanced by the glass side and coffee tables. And on the opposite wall from the black chairs, the dark walnut piano matches the visual weight of the chairs, creating an overall balanced look and keeping the room from feeling lopsided.

Cowhide-Covered Piano Bench

Speaking of the dark walnut piano, when I scored this vintage beauty a few years ago, the bench was pretty worn and weathered. So much so that I initially put it on my furniture edit list and considered replacing it with something new. It was clear that this piano and matching bench had seen a lot of love and use over the years. Though I knew Restor-A-Finish could work its magic on the piano (see page 153 for a brief description), the bench was just too far gone. So, onto my edit list it went.

But here is yet another example of finding creative freedom and permission to play with your edit list. You see, in addition to this bench looking extremely rough and worn, I felt that the dark bench against the dark piano was also a bit too visually heavy. And though at this point in my life I had never yet stripped a piece of furniture, my how-hard-can-it-be gene—coupled with the fact that I had nothing to lose because this bench was on my edit list—propelled me to experiment. The result is a piece of furniture that I still love! The lighter wood combined with the cowhide-upholstered seat made this tired old piano bench feel fresh enough to be crossed off my edit list for good.

This DIY furniture project is proof that no previous experience is necessary to strip an old piece of furniture.

SUPPLIES NEEDED

–Cleaning supplies

–Safety gloves

–Paint and varnish stripper
  (Most brands of stripper will remove latex and oil-based, enamel and acrylic paints, and varnish. I prefer to use those that come in a spray can.)

–Plastic wrap

–Plastic scraper

–Power sander or medium-grit sanding block

–Stain brush

–Wood stain

–Foam brush

–Minwax Polycrylic protective finish (This clear topcoat protects against scratches and scuffs.)

–Cowhide

–Staple gun

QUICK TIP

Paint and varnish stripper stops working when it dries, so I recommend wrapping your furniture with plastic wrap after applying the stripper, working in sections until your piece is completely covered. This will allow the stripper to stay wet and thereby remain active, which will make stain removal so much easier, especially in any carved areas!

QUICK TIP

For the best results, I recommend waiting about 24 hours after stripping a piece of furniture before applying any stain or sealer.

STEP-BY-STEP PROCESS

Step 1: Start by giving your bench (or whatever piece of furniture you are stripping) a good cleaning. Be sure to wear protective gloves as you apply the stripper to your cleaned furniture. Next, wrap the piece with plastic wrap. (Keep in mind, the chemical process works best above 50 degrees Fahrenheit.)

Step 2: After waiting about 4 to 6 hours (sometimes I wait a full 24 hours, depending on how dark of a stain I am removing) for the paint and varnish stripper to do its job, remove the plastic wrap and marvel at how the layers of stain are easily removed with your plastic scraper.

Step 3: Use your power sander or medium-grit sanding block to finish removing the stain.

Step 4: Using a stain brush, apply your chosen wood stain. (I used a mix of three stain colors to get the finish I wanted.)

Step 5: Once your stain is completely dry, use a foam brush to apply a coat of Minwax Polycrylic.

Step 6 (Optional): Wrap the bench seat with cowhide or a small rug, and use a staple gun to attach it to the underside of the bench.

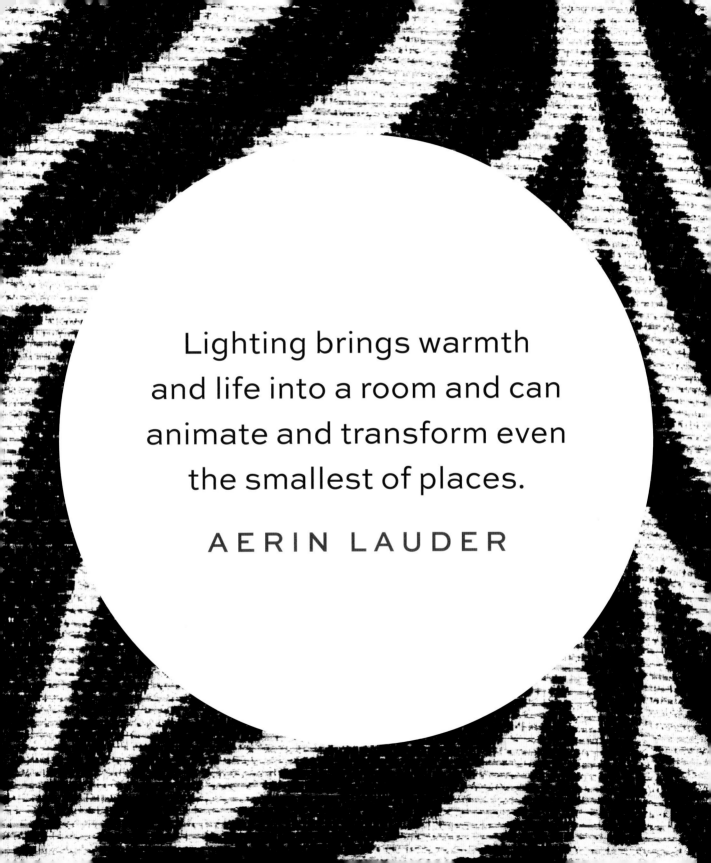

Lighting brings warmth
and life into a room and can
animate and transform even
the smallest of places.

AERIN LAUDER

CHAPTER SIX

Adding Sparkle With Lighting

I f there is a design element I believe is splurge-worthy, it is without question lighting! Just as an outfit is not complete without jewelry, a room is not finished without lighting. This, my friends, is another design truth: Lighting is *everything*! Lighting is the jewelry in a room, during both the day and at night. But of course, at night especially, lighting is a key player in setting the mood. And lamp o'clock is my favorite time of day!

I hate to say that lighting can make or break the entire design of a room—because that sounds super dramatic—but I think deep down we both know it's true. If you have ever lived in a home with any of those infamous builder-grade flushmount light fixtures, I think you know what I'm talking about here. It's not just me, right? We all feel like replacing one of those fixtures is a spiritual experience. I'm pretty sure I can hear angels singing every time.

In all seriousness, though, the power of great lighting should never be underestimated, as nothing transforms a space quicker than replacing outdated fixtures! Light fixtures bring in a lot of visual design bang for the buck while also doing some serious heavy lifting. They work hard in a space, obviously combining form with function. Not only do they check the much-needed illumination box in a home, but light fixtures also bring in that oh-so-special sparkle that completes a space like nothing else can.

Now, I'm not speaking of sparkle in a literal sense here, although I absolutely live for the twinkle and glow of a crystal chandelier. Rather, I see the sparkle that light fixtures add to a room as the icing on a cake. Lighting is the design element in a room that can really make a space feel, in a word, *memorable.* It is the light fixtures in a space that can really invite you in, often commanding attention, while providing the perfect opportunity to let your unique design vibe truly shine. Pun intended.

Hardwired fixtures like chandeliers, pendants, and sconces can absolutely give a home personality, but the impact of lamps and lampshades should not be overlooked. Lighting in all its forms and facets has the power to transform a space in mere seconds. And there are beautiful options to suit every budget. Fashion icon Iris Apfel once said, "An outfit is only as good as the accessories you pair it with." And I believe this sentiment translates to interior design as well. A room is only as good as the light fixtures you outfit it with.

Most of us likely have zero trouble selecting a single fixture—say, a chandelier to hang over our dining room table. When you know the design vibe you want for your home, choosing one fixture you love

is simple enough. The hurdle often arises when we look at the larger picture of outfitting an *entire home* with light fixtures. That is when a myriad of questions might come up.

How do you coordinate lighting throughout a home? How do you know what size lampshade to use? Should all the lampshades in a room match? Why do I love the paint color on my living room walls during the day but hate it at night? Could it perhaps have something to do with the light bulbs I'm using?

These are some of the most common lighting questions I've been asked over the years. And the good news is, there are a few lessons, guidelines, and tips that once learned can really help you to answer these questions for yourself and confidently outfit your whole home with light fixtures that speak to your design vibe. The goal with lighting is to make your home look, function, and *feel* its best during the day and at night. So, let's uncover the sparkle of lighting!

The Three Basic Types (Layers) of Light

The best way to light up a home, just like the best way to make a chocolate cake, is to do it in layers. There are three basic layers to a lighting scheme: ambient, accent, and task.

Ambient

Ambient lighting is often referred to as general lighting. It's what gives a room an overall glow. This type of lighting is mostly overhead or recessed, but it can be any lighting that provides a lot of light in a room in a diffused way.

This is admittedly less of a tip and more of a recommendation or personal mantra, if you will. Nonetheless, I refer to overhead fixtures and recessed lighting as "the big lights" in a space, and I believe you will never regret putting these lights on dimmer switches. A dimmer switch is surprisingly simple to install yourself (if I can do it, anyone can!) and costs roughly twenty dollars at the hardware store. And I promise you, this twenty-dollar upgrade is a game changer! The ability to control the output of light from "the big lights" in a room will absolutely change the way you use and feel about the overhead lighting in your home, no matter what your design vibe is, but especially so for all of you cozy home lovers. Trust me!

Battery-operated sconces and picture lights can be your best friend in places where hardwiring isn't an option or an outlet is unavailable.

Accent

Accent lighting can be useful, but this type of lighting is mostly about bringing in some decorative or visual interest to a space. Accent lights serve as, well, accent pieces—hence the name. They are not used or needed to illuminate an entire room but rather are meant to highlight special features like architectural details, art, and bookcases in a room. I like to think of accent lighting as spotlights that shine a light on the notable stars in a room. Examples include picture lights over artwork, lighting in sconces, and lights in glass cabinets.

Task

Task lighting is used for exactly what it sounds like. It's lighting that is used for specific tasks. These are typically smaller light fixtures that are placed strategically to provide light for activities like reading. A floor lamp in a cozy reading corner and a desk lamp are examples of task lighting.

While using all three types of lighting in a space is an excellent idea, not every room requires all three. You need not stress over creating the perfect mix of ambient, accent, and task lighting. The main takeaway here and

what is truly the most important thing to remember when it comes to lighting is that every room needs at least two to three sources of light. If you focus on that, you will inevitably include at least two of the three types of lighting in every room.

In a living room, for example, you might have an overhead light or recessed lights then add sconces or a picture light and finally a table or floor lamp. The key is having a variety of light sources that spread light in various places and at different heights around a room. Layering lighting well in a room is not only about including multiple sources or types of light; it is also very much about distributing light throughout a room.

I also believe that light *bulbs* are extremely important as well, but we will chat more about that later in this chapter. First, now that we've covered the three different layers of light, let's jump in to mixing and matching fixtures for a coordinated look throughout a home.

Coordinating Light Fixtures Throughout a Home

Whether you live in an open-concept home where multiple light fixtures are within view of one another or you are in a home where most of your rooms have four walls, coordinating light fixtures throughout your home can make your home feel more cohesive. We chatted about house flow in chapter 2 as paint and specifically color plays a significant role in creating flow from room to room. However, lighting should not be overlooked in this area, as it is also a key player. When done well, lighting can create a whole-home cohesive feel, tying spaces together and reinforcing your overall design vibe. The primary goal is to curate light fixtures that flow (or as I like to say, play well together) rather than using fixtures that look like they all came from the same lighting collection.

When selecting light fixtures for my own home, I aim to convey one overall lighting story throughout my home while allowing for each fixture to write its own chapter. Does this make sense? Essentially, I want every fixture to feel like a unique piece of the lighting puzzle where they are all special and unique, and they all fit together.

If you are building, renovating, or selecting several new light fixtures at one time it can be helpful to create a mood board to visualize how all the fixtures will relate to one another.

The best interior designers make coordinating light fixtures throughout a home look effortless, but a great deal of effort and intention is involved in carefully crafting a lighting plan. However, I do not believe you have to go to design school to do this well in your own home. The key to coordinating light fixtures throughout a home is to select light fixtures that relate to one another in either style, material, or finish. Emphasis on the word *or*. So long as you hit at least one of those categories, your light fixtures will play well together. And it is even better if they also tie in to other design elements in the room in some way.

In my kitchen, for example, the polished brass pendants over the island play nicely with the polished brass backplate and arm of the sconces over the windows, while the brass finish ties into the cabinet hardware. The light blue metal sconce shades tie into the color of the kitchen island cabinets. The fixtures relate to one another with their brass finish and classic style, and they relate to other design elements in the space as well.

The same is true in my pantry, which is within view of the kitchen, where the polished brass pendant plays well with both the island

The key to coordi-
nating light fixtures
throughout a home is
to select light fixtures
that relate to one
another in either style,
material, or finish.

pendants and the sconces. Even the brass neck and finial of the chinoiserie lamp on the counter relates to the pendant, while the blue of the lamp base complements the cabinets, and the red lampshade ties in with both the rug in the pantry and the runner in the kitchen.

The modern style of the light fixture in my living room contrasts a bit with the style of the fixtures in my kitchen, but the brass finish allows them to play well with one another. As long as one design element ties fixtures together, they will coordinate. And bonus points are added when the fixtures relate to another design element in the space similarly to the way the black metal shades of my living room fixture tie in with the windows, sliding doors, and chairs.

What About Mixing Metals?

It's a yes for me! Maybe it's because a mixed-metal look lends itself to a collected feel, and that is totally my design vibe. I love mixing metals throughout my home. Whenever people ask about whether all the light fixtures throughout a home need to have the same metal finish to coordinate well or create a cohesive feel, I always give a resounding no as my answer. You are totally allowed to hang an oil-rubbed bronze lantern in your entry foyer and have brass or chrome light fixtures in your kitchen.

Not to sound like a broken record, but it bears repeating: So long as fixtures relate in either style, material, *or* finish, they will play well with one another. Does that oil-rubbed bronze lantern have a modern style? Then select modern-style light fixtures for your kitchen. Or does that lantern have seeded glass? Then maybe opt for kitchen light fixtures that have seeded glass components. Creating a cohesive lighting plan for a home is more of an art than a science. Trust your eye, and keep in mind that you have room to play with fixtures that are not within view of one another.

When people ask about mixing metal finishes with light fixtures, often what they are really inquiring about is how to mix metal finishes in spaces like bathrooms and kitchens, where you also need to consider things like cabinet hardware and plumbing fixtures. I believe no matter what your design vibe is, mixed metals bring in a layered look that adds both depth and interest. Here are a few tips for achieving a beautifully layered mixed-metal look:

- **Go for contrast**. The goal is for your mix of metal finishes to look intentional, and choosing metals from different color categories allows this to happen. As an example, rather than mixing chrome with satin nickel, opt for more contrast by mixing chrome with aged brass. Mixing cool tones with warm ones creates contrast and balance. Plus, the end result looks like the finishes were chosen purposefully.
- **Select a dominant metal finish**. Two or a maximum of three metal finishes work well in a space when one metal finish dominates or leads the mixed-metal story. In a bathroom or kitchen, consider choosing one finish for both the lighting and cabinet hardware and using another finish for the mirrors or faucets.

- **Keep metals with the same function consistent**. Interior designers often phrase this tip as "keeping the metals within the same viewing plane consistent," but I have found that to be a little confusing. Sometimes in a kitchen, for example, you might have tall upper cabinets with hardware that is within the same viewing eyeline as the pendants over your island, but that does not necessarily mean the metal finishes need to match. I prefer the idea of matching the metal finish of items that have the same function. In a bathroom, for example, all the plumbing fixtures—sink faucet, shower head, tub spout, and the like—would all be in the same finish.
- **When in doubt, go for black**. Brass, chrome, nickel, and bronze are beautiful metal finishes, but nothing is easier to effortlessly mix in to a space than black! It's the perfect neutral metal finish that quite literally goes with everything. So, if you are feeling intimidated, opt for black. It will give you the contrast, depth, and interest while adding a modern touch.

As always, there are exceptions. These tips are meant to be inspiring not restricting. In addition, there is no rule that says you must mix metal finishes. There are lots of ways to add contrast and interest to a space outside of mixing metals. For the main bathroom in our home, I opted to stick to chrome for the plumbing fixtures, cabinet hardware, and light fixtures, bringing in contrast via other design elements like the black cabinets and shower tile. To balance the cool tones and add in some much-needed warmth, I opted to bring in warm browns via an area rug and wood-framed mirrors. I sprinkled in a few small brass decorative accessories, but this is predominantly a one-metal finish space. And it feels anything but lackluster to me. So mix metals if you want to, but do not feel obligated.

Don't Forget About Lamps

So far, we have mostly focused on hardwired or battery-operated light fixtures, but lamps are my love language. Whenever I have helped family and friends with decorating projects in their homes, the first thing I notice is that their spaces could use more lamps. Lamps are so often overlooked. And it's a shame really, because they make styling so much easier. We will chat more in depth about styling in the next chapter, but when you use one or two lamps on a console or sideboard, you really do not need to use much more in the decorative accessories department to complete the vignette. In this way, lamps are a great styling hack!

Even with most of "the big lights" in my home on dimmer switches, I almost never use them at night. Lamp light is so much cozier. However, as much as I appreciate the cozy factor that lamps bring in during the evening, I love the personality and style they add to a space no matter the time of day. I see them as useful, sculptural pieces of art, and I love to use them anywhere and everywhere I can. My motto for pretty much any and all flat surfaces in my home is "put a lamp on it." I just love the visual interest that lamps add to a space. I'm especially fond of them in places where they feel a bit unexpected, like kitchens, bathrooms, and laundry rooms. They make for wonderful night lights in those spaces.

The beauty of online shopping is that it has truly made good design much more accessible and affordable. No matter your budget or your design vibe, you can easily source fantastic lamp options.

QUICK TIP

If you want to add a lamp to a spot where you don't have a nearby outlet, use a rechargeable light bulb. Remote-controlled light bulbs last for hours before needing to be recharged and are not only great for decor purposes but they come in handy during power outages as well. I keep one in my entry foyer lamp and in the lamp in our powder room. (I love keeping a lamp on in a powder room so guests feel welcome.)

Secondhand for the Win

I love online shopping, but I will always advocate for vintage lamps. I jokingly tell people that thrifting is my cardio, but it's partially true. Many items in my home were purchased secondhand. I'm a big believer that one person's trash is another's treasure. Vintage lamps— well, they just don't make lamps like they used to, you know? As I write this chapter, nine of the eighteen lamps on my first floor were thrifted, most for under thirty dollars. So all I'm saying is, don't skip the thrift! There are treasures to be found at thrift stores and on Facebook Marketplace. Most just need a new lampshade or could use a coat of paint (see the DIY Spotlight at the end of this chapter).

Mix Shades or Match Shades?

There is no wrong answer here. This is completely relative to your design vibe and your unique space. All the lampshades in a room do not need to match unless that is your preference. If each shade relates to the room in some way, using a mix of lampshades is not only fine but lovely. Because my design vibe is collected, a mix of shades works well in my home. If you love a clean, minimalist design vibe, you might opt for all white lampshades.

Selecting the Right Size Lampshade

Choosing the perfectly sized lampshade is fairly simple. There are just two easy-to-remember ~~rules~~ guidelines that you will want to follow.

1. You want the width of the shade to be double the size of the base.

2. You want the height of the shade to be about a third of the total height of the lamp, including the harp (give or take a few inches).

No need to stress over exact measurements. After all, rules are meant to be broken. The only thing that truly matters is keeping the lamp harp (or the working parts of the lamp) fully covered by the shade.

The Only Design Rule I Truly Follow: An Ode to 2700 Kelvin

This is the only section of the book where I am going to put on my bossy pants. But I'm doing it out of love, friends, because I believe everyone deserves to live their absolute best lamp o'clock life. As readers of my blog and my Instagram community know, I have big opinions about light bulb temperatures. If lamps are my love language, 2700 kelvin is my religion. Warm light is the best light. I said what I said. This is more than a design truth; it is a design fact. That said, I do think it is acceptable to veer into slightly cooler light bulb temperatures in spaces like bathrooms, kitchens, closets, and laundry rooms. Utilitarian spaces can often benefit from neutral as opposed to warm light. Even so, just about every light bulb in my home is 2700 kelvin.

It is honestly surprising to me that light bulb temperature is not discussed more within the design community. Because lighting is, as I've already mentioned, everything; but at

QUICK TIP

An adjustable lamp harp can be the perfect fix when the height of a lampshade just isn't looking quite right. This will allow you to easily raise or lower the shade for the perfect height.

night, light *bulbs* are 80 percent of the game. And if they are not done right, if they are not 2700K, you might as well throw all your lamps and light fixtures away. In all seriousness, I came across my love of 2700 kelvin the hard way.

Once upon a time, I repainted my entire living room because the paint color on the walls at night looked so cold and harsh. Come to find out (after repainting the whole space and disliking the new color just as much as the one I had just painted over), the problem was my light bulbs, not the paint color. That was a fun lesson. Thankfully, an especially helpful gentleman in the paint department showed me the light, literally and figuratively—pun obviously intended. This was house number three. I shudder to tell you, I was using daylight bulbs. 5000 kelvin. Gulp! As soon as I switched my lamps to my now beloved 2700K light bulbs, all was right in not just my living room but my entire world. And so began my love affair with warm light bulb temperatures.

My proudest mom moment to date was the day I helped my son move into his first apartment, and he asked me to "please change all the light bulbs to 2700 kelvin." What can I say? I raised him right. Unfortunately, the language of light bulbs is not taught in schools. Instead, we learn about super important things like parallelograms. So, because the light bulb aisle can be a little intimidating and there are numbers, phrases, and words on the boxes that might be foreign to you, I thought a concise rundown might be helpful.

The Language of Light Bulbs

- It's an easy language to learn! There are two basic terms you need to know: *lumens* and *kelvins*.

- **Lumens** are about brightness or how much light a bulb will give. More lumens equal more light.
- **Kelvins** are about temperature. How warm (yellow) or cool (blue) a bulb is depends on the kelvin number. Higher numbers are cooler than lower numbers. So 3000K is cooler than 2700K.

QUICK TIP

If you are a warm light lover, try amber glass light bulbs, and thank me later.

Color Temperatures of Light Bulbs

2200–2700K	Soft warm light similar to an incandescent bulb (anything under 2700K almost mimics the glow of candlelight)	Great for bedrooms, living rooms, dining rooms, entry foyers, hallways, and even outdoor spaces
3000–3500K	Bright white light	Great for kitchens, bathrooms, offices, and laundry rooms
4000–5000K	Cool light	Only good for garages

Painted Lampshade

As I mentioned earlier, sometimes all an old, thrifted lampshade needs is a coat of paint. And painting a lampshade is a very beginner-friendly DIY. It's a good trick to pull out whenever you are ready for a slight change in your space but do not want to spend a lot of money. In addition, painting a lampshade is a great noncommittal way to experiment with color! In about thirty minutes or so you can give an old fabric lampshade a fun makeover.

A few years ago, I bought a vintage lamp for my daughter's room. While the shade was in good condition, the beige color felt a bit too boring for her bedroom. A quick coat of pink paint remedied the situation perfectly, giving this shade a sweet touch of whimsy.

SUPPLIES NEEDED

–Drop cloth (to protect your work surface)
–Acrylic craft paint
–Bowl (for mixing the paint)
–Foam paintbrush

STEP-BY-STEP PROCESS

Step 1: Prepare your workspace with a drop cloth, then start by mixing your paint with water to create a soup-like mixture that is not too thick or too thin. You want a consistency that will drip. The goal is for the paint to go on more like a stain than a paint so that the paint is absorbed by the fabric.

Step 2: Using your foam paintbrush, apply one coat of paint. (A foam brush allows for a nice, streak-free finish.)

Step 3: Depending on the color you have selected and how deep you want the color to be, additional coats may be needed. For an even finish, just be sure to let each coat dry thoroughly before applying another coat.

QUICK TIP

It is easiest to paint the shade while it is attached to the lamp base, but you may want to cover the base with a cloth or plastic bag to catch any paint drips.

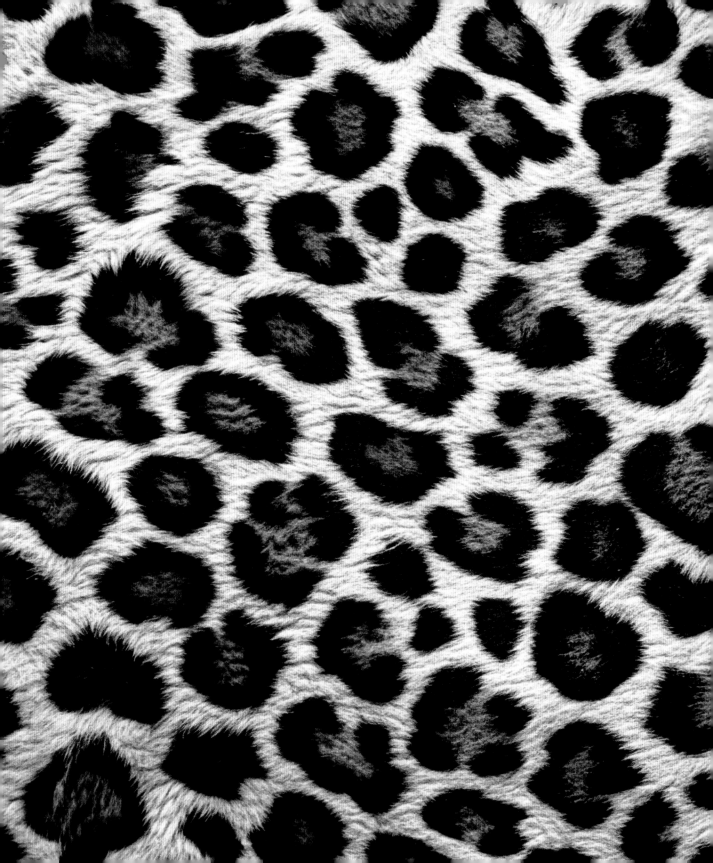

It doesn't have to be
perfect to be beautiful.

MYQUILLYN SMITH

We all need a splash of
bad taste; no taste
is what I am against.

— Diana Vreeland

CHAPTER SEVEN

Bringing It All Together Through Styling

Styling is my favorite part of design since I have always lived for the details in a space. For me it's the little things in a home, the decorative accessories, that say so much about the people who dwell within its walls. The design lover and curious house guest in me absolutely loves to peruse the vignettes—mantels, coffee tables, bookcases—in a person's home. From the number of items to the tchotchkes themselves to the way each item is displayed or arranged, it gives me a beautiful glimpse at who a person is. I believe the decorative accessories we collect and choose to exhibit say more about us than any other design element in our homes.

Whether you are a maximalist or a minimalist, design is truly in the details. And that can be both inspiring and intimidating. Collecting things is a lot easier than styling the things we have collected. However, the good news is twofold:

1. Styling is a skill. So, anyone can learn to do it well!
2. As Myquillyn Smith, The Nester, says, "It doesn't have to be perfect to be beautiful."

That second point feels so freeing, right? I specifically chose to start this chapter with that encouraging quote because, more than any other aspect of decorating, styling seems to be the area that causes the most frustration. But I promise, it is not just you. Arranging stuff is simply not that easy. I mean, it's not rocket science, but it also is not something you are born knowing how to do. Sure, there are the artists and innately stylish among us who come by decorative styling a bit more easily than others, but for the most part, styling is like riding a bike. It is something we must learn.

Embarrassing but true, I did not learn how to ride a bike until the fifth grade. Yes, I was a ten-year-old with training wheels on her bike. Until one day my dad decided the best way to help me get over my fear was to shove me into the face of danger by removing my trusty training wheels and taking me to a huge empty parking lot where no one was around to hear me screaming. (Also, just to paint the picture

accurately for you, I'm a child of the pre-helmet and kneepad era. So there's that.) Am I scarred both physically and emotionally from that experience? Uh, is there a Gen Xer alive today who doesn't have some scars from their childhood? I learned two things that day besides finally learning how to ride a bike:

1. We may learn differently, but we all learn.
2. Falling is not failing, but asphalt is no one's friend.

(P.S. Every time my almost-eighty-year-old dad comes to visit me, we go on a bike ride around my neighborhood together, and I'm grateful I can ride without those training wheels.)

Styling, like riding a bike, is a skill that, once you have learned, becomes muscle memory. And the more you do it, the better you become. But the learning process can be a journey. Maybe not a ten-year-old-with-training-wheels kind of journey, but nonetheless, there may be some wobbles, scrapes, and bruises along the way. As someone who has been documenting her decorating adventures online for more than twelve years, I can honestly tell you that sometimes I cringe at the styling in some of my oldest photos. But I'm glad I kept pedaling. Styling isn't about making it perfect; it's about making it beautiful. And those are two different things.

So, let's take the training wheels off and have some fun with styling! At least we won't have to worry about hitting the pavement.

Bookshelves: A Don't-Miss Decorating Opportunity

Let's start with bookshelves. Styling shelves and bookcases can feel a bit overwhelming, but they present the perfect opportunity for you to have a little show-and-tell moment in your home. I like to think of shelves as the perfect platform to shine a light on the little things that matter to you. When it comes to styling shelves, I think too often there is too much attention focused on how you want them to look and not enough time spent thinking about what you want them to say. Obviously, you want your arrangement of items to look beautiful, but what do you want the arrangement to convey? Do you have any special interests, hobbies, or collections? It can be helpful to reflect on your design vibe words before you begin styling.

The stylists for brands like Pottery Barn, Ballard Designs, and Serena & Lily, to name a few, are amazing. Like me, I'm sure a lot of you love slowly flipping through those catalogs, preferably with an iced coffee in hand. But I think it's important to keep in mind that styling in home decor catalogues is mostly done with the intent to sell us something, not to tell us anything personal about the people who reside in those impeccably beautiful images. They are styling spaces for the masses—not for individuals with unique stories to tell. The bookshelves in your home should reflect your people and your story—not necessarily your favorite home store.

That is not to say you shouldn't display store-bought accessories (I have lots of those!). I rather want to remind you that it is more than okay to add *life* to your bookshelves in addition to the pretty things you've purchased from home decor stores. Include the weird stuff, the sentimental pieces, and the pieces that might spark conversation. Your shelves will be so much more personal and interesting if you display the sweet but wonky-looking clay piece your child made for you or your dad's dog tag from when he served in Vietnam. Let your shelves tell people something about who you are. Don't miss this

Your shelves will be so much more personal and interesting if you display the sweet but wonky-looking clay piece your child made for you or your dad's dog tag from when he served in Vietnam.

incredible opportunity in your home to beautifully share your story through your decorating.

My Five-Step Process to Styling Bookshelves

I live, laugh, love to style bookshelves! And I promise my five-step process will have you living, laughing, and loving it too! Five steps might make this sound complicated but I promise it is not. Whether you are in a styling slump or just ready to give your bookshelves a fresh look, my easy-to-follow process will hopefully spark your creativity and get you into a shelfie-styling groove.

QUICK TIP

Run through this process *before* you run to the store. Shopping your home first will set you up for success. It allows you to see exactly where the "holes" are—the places on your shelves where you need or want a new piece—so you can shop with more purpose and intention. When you start with what you have you can chart a much clearer path forward. Bonus, this also pushes you to bust out the cool, weird, wonky, personal stuff that will give your shelves a unique, interesting look.

Step 1: Clear the Bookshelves

If you have just moved into a new-to-you home and are starting with a clean slate, perfect! But don't hate me if your shelves are filled and you just want to freshen them up a bit. Sorry, I'm not sorry: No matter what, I always recommend starting with empty shelves. It might feel like a pain to remove everything on your shelves and start from scratch, but this step is so key! Clearing your bookshelves allows you to see them with fresh eyes. It's the perfect reset to get you into a creative head space.

Step 2: Cast Your Bookshelves

Admittedly, this step is a bit of an abstract idea, but just go with me here. This is where you take a step back, examine the room as a whole, and decide if you want your bookshelves to be the star of the show—the thing that draws the most attention in your room—or if you want them to function as a beautiful backdrop, playing more of a supporting role. Do you want your bookshelves to have main-character energy or would you rather them win the award for best supporting actress? There is no wrong answer here. This step is meant to help you gain some clarity regarding what items and more specifically what colors you want to use in your display. Figuring out how you want your bookshelves to act in your space sets you up for success with steps three and four.

Step 3: Create a Color Story

Your color story will obviously be based off the colors in your space, and it can be as wide (including lots of colors) or as tight (just two or three colors) as you would like it to be. Typically, the wider the color palette the more eclectic and collected as well as attention-grabbing (main-character energy) your display will look, whereas a tighter palette of just two or three colors will convey more of a clean and simple vibe that is a bit more subtle in your space (supporting role). Again, there is no wrong answer, but reflecting on both your design vibe and the role you want your bookshelves to play in your space will help you to decide on a color story.

Step 4: Gather All the Things

Now, you are ready to start gathering your accessories. Think books, boxes, bowls, vases, candlesticks, trays, baskets, small works of art—the more the merrier when it comes to rounding up decor. However, you only want to gather what fits your color story. And

the goal is to gather more items than you will need, so when you are styling your shelves, you have lots of options right at your fingertips from which to choose.

Step 5: Host Auditions

This is my favorite step of the process! I feel like it's the grown-up decorating version of playing dress-up, and the drama queen in me enjoys referring to this part of the process as hosting auditions. There really is no better way to describe this step! This is where you play with all the things you've gathered, and you move things around until you find the exact right pieces and the exact right arrangement. You audition each piece until you find your cast of accessories.

QUICK TIP

As you gather, group accessories by color to make the styling process less chaotic. This will really come in handy when you start arranging items on your shelves (more on that in the "Styling Tips" section).

This step can take a *long* time. Take a deep breath, put on your favorite Taylor Swift album, or rent an audiobook from the library (how did we ever live without the Libby app?), and enjoy the process. Have fun arranging your treasures. Look at your bookshelves the way you looked at a brand-new box of crayons when you were young and get excited to decorate! Here are some styling tips and ideas to help you get started:

Bookshelf Styling Tips

- **Start with books.** I always start with books, whether I am using a lot of them or just a few of them. In my opinion, every bookshelf, whether intended to store books or not, should have at least a few books. When it comes to styling, they make for a great jumping-off point. I like to stagger them throughout a bookshelf, alternating between stacking them horizontally and vertically.

- **Put the best things at the top and at eye level**. Once I have added books, I focus my attention on the top shelves and then move to those that are at eye level, using my most treasured pieces here since these are the shelves the eye is naturally drawn to first.

- **Go big on top and bottom and little in the middle**. Smaller items are not easily visible on shelves above eye level, and on floor-to-ceiling bookcases they tend to get lost when placed on bottom shelves. Using larger pieces on the top and bottom shelves creates a visually balanced look and allows the eye to appreciate each accessory. Layering in your smaller pieces at eye level keeps them from being overlooked.

- **Little things often need anchors**. Even at eye level, smaller accessories can get lost in the shuffle and end up looking more like cluttered chaos than an intentional display. Using trays, baskets, or even books to corral little things quiets the chaos. It gives a group or even just one small item a much-needed anchor.

- **Three's company**. No, I'm not talking about Jack, Janet, and Chrissy. I'm referring to the Rule of Three in design, which suggests that things look best grouped in threes. Odd numbers tend to be more visually appealing. But do not let this rule restrict you. Use it as a guideline and break it on purpose. As an example, on my living room shelves I have grouped two large bowls instead of three smaller bowls

because these two bowls fill up the space and are so similar that they appear to make one large statement.

- **Create movement with color.** I like to repeat colors at least three times, creating visual triangles to keep the eye moving and create visual balance. (This is why, as I mentioned earlier, I like to group my accessories by color when I am gathering items.)
- **Mix in plenty of round and sculptural objects.** This breaks up all the straight lines and adds some nice contrast and tension.
- **Layer in art.** It adds depth and interest.
- **Say yes to glass.** Clear glass items add sparkle and subtle contrast, giving the eye a quiet, yet interesting place to rest.
- **Blank space isn't bad.** Speaking of giving the eye a place to rest, don't feel like you need to fill every nook and cranny.
- **Take a picture.** When you are done playing decor dress-up, step back and take a picture of your styled shelves. This allows you to see the shelves as a whole, whereas in real life your eyes tend to focus on one area. The picture can help you to see where you might want to make any final tweaks.

QUICK TIP

Books can be art too! I love using easels to display special books.

A Novel Idea: Just Use Books

To steal a sentiment from Miranda Priestly: Books? On bookshelves? Groundbreaking. But I think sometimes as decor enthusiasts we can feel pressured to place more than just books on our shelves. But as a reader, a lover of books in a home, and someone who believes in letting your shelves tell your story, nothing is more beautiful or personal to me than a shelf filled with only books. And from a styling perspective, it does not get any easier. So, if bookshelf styling is just not your cup of tea, let your shelves drown in books.

But as a reader, a lover of books in a home, and someone who believes in letting your shelves tell your story, nothing is more beautiful or personal to me than a shelf filled with only books.

Coffee Tables: Beautiful and Functional

Coffee tables are workhorses in a home, and I prefer to style mine with accessories that combine beauty and function. I think it's important to consider how you use your coffee table before you begin styling. Do you set drinks down on your table? Is this where you want to store the television remote? Are you a candle person, a plant person, or both? Do you like to keep a pair of reading glasses nearby? Does your table get used for games or crafts? A beautifully styled coffee table is great, but one that is both beautiful and functional is golden.

Coffee Table Styling Tips

- **Work in sections**. Creating a grid or dividing the surface area into quadrants makes the task of decorating a large, flat surface feel more manageable. My square living room coffee table, as an example, has four sections. An oval table might have two or three. And a round table's sections might look more like a triangle.
- **Vary the heights**. When everything on a coffee table is at the same height, nothing draws in the eye and all the accessories

sort of blend together. Varying the height keeps the eye moving and feels more dynamic.

- **Bring in decorative storage**. Because why not? A vintage shell box to house remotes? Yes, please!
- **Leave intentional open space in trays, baskets, or bowls**. Failing to plan is planning to fail. If you tend to leave your reading glasses, current book, or recent magazines on your coffee table, why not style your table with a tray, basket, or bowl to designate a spot for these items? That way they look like an intentional part of your decor rather than clutter.

Mantels: Drive Home Your Design Vibe

A fireplace is often the focal point in a space, so a mantel presents the perfect place to drive home your unique design vibe. It is also a great spot to revisit throughout the year to keep your space feeling fresh as the seasons change.

Mantel Styling Tips

QUICK TIP

If you are placing a mirror above your mantel, remember to consider what will be reflected. If it's a beautiful light fixture or a great piece of art from across the room, wonderful! If it's your necessary-but-not-so-pretty ceiling fan, maybe go for a piece of art above your mantel instead.

- **Start with an anchor piece**. The focal point in the room needs a great focal piece, like a mirror, clock, wall basket, wreath, or a large piece of art. I'm a major fan of the Samsung Frame TV, as it combines form with function and allows me to change the art displayed as often as I would like. However, if you have a traditional black

box television above your mantel, you could hang your focal point above your TV if the ceiling height allows.

- **Balance the sides**. Adding visual weight to both sides of your mantel creates balance and adds dimension. I love using candlesticks and a vase or large planter, as these are pieces that are easy to tweak for a fresh look throughout the year without having to reinvent the ~~wheel~~ mantel.

- **Add some fillers or layers**. Smaller pieces add personality and bring in both texture and a variety of heights.

QUICK TIP

If you are working around a black box TV, matching pieces like lanterns, vases, or sconces bring in a visually pleasing symmetrical look that draws attention away from the TV.

Sideboards, Buffets, and Console Tables: Just Add Lamps

When it comes to styling sideboards, buffets, and console tables, I'm on team lamp. I mentioned this in the last chapter, but adding a lamp or two to these pieces of furniture takes a lot of the styling guesswork out of the equation because lamps have so much visual presence that you do not need much more in the way of decorative accessories. Matching lamps? Just add a stack of books or boxes between the lamps and call her good. Going for an asymmetrical look using just one lamp? Balance the visual weight of the lamp on the other end of the table and add some decorative accessories, à la the way you might style a mantel. The key is to bring in lamps.

We all need a splash of bad taste; no taste is what I am against

– Diana Vreeland

photos

THE FASHION FILE   Jane Bryant

Expressionism

IMPRESSIONISM AND
POST-IMPRESSIONISM

KELDER   The Great Book of
French Impressionism

Faux Burl Wood Box

Boxes, if you haven't already noticed, are some of my favorite decor accessories to use in my home. I'm all about beautiful storage. Burl wood is another design love of mine, but burl wood accessories often come with a hefty price tag. So, a few years ago, when I stumbled across some burl wood contact paper on Amazon, I jumped at the chance to make some boxes with it. (However, if burl wood isn't your jam, any contact paper or peel-and-stick wallpaper will work for this quick DIY decor project.)

SUPPLIES NEEDED

–Craft wood box
–Burl wood contact paper or any patterned contact paper or peel-and-stick wallpaper you like.
–Black Sharpie marker
–Scissors
–Wallpaper smoothing tool
–Foam paintbrush
–Mod Podge

STEP-BY-STEP PROCESS

Step 1: Lay each section of the box down on the reverse side of the contact paper and carefully trace around each section with a Sharpie.

Step 2: Carefully cut out the box pattern you created.

Step 3: Use a Sharpie to darken the edges of the box, so seams will be less noticeable.

Step 4: Piece by piece, remove the plastic backing and adhere the cut pieces to the box using the smoothing tool to work out any air bubbles.

Step 5: Using a foam paintbrush, add a light coat of Mod Podge all over the box to seal down the edges and prevent peeling.

Step 6: Marvel at how real your faux burl wood box looks!

Favorite Design Sources

Many items in my home have either been thrifted or handmade, but here's a source list for everything else.

Entry Foyer

Table – LexMod
Rug – CB2
Striped Art – Artist, Angela Chrusciaki Blehm

Dining Room

Striped Grasscloth Wallpaper – Spoonflower
Slipcovered Dining Chairs – The Inside
Crystal Chandelier – Crystorama
Trophy Table Lamps – Pottery Barn
Ceramic Bow – Artist, Maryfrances Carter

Living Room

Rug – Lulu & Georgia
Black & White Chair – West Elm
Sofa – Restoration Hardware
Stools – Ballard Designs

Rattan Side Tables – Studio McGee for Target
Console Table – Pottery Barn
Wicker Lamp Shade – Ballard Designs
Mirror – Anthropologie
Floral Abstract – Artist, Carrie Davis

Kitchen

Cabinet Hardware – Atlas Hardware
Sconces – Rejuvenation
Pendants – Restoration Hardware
Faucet – Perrin and Rowe
Runner – Zuma Imports
Abstract Floral Art – painted by my mom

Pantry

Pendant – Rejuvenation

Laundry Room

Wallpaper – Spoonflower

Black & White Art – Vibrant Vintage Prints on Etsy

Floral Portrait Print – Artist, Clare Elsaesser

Pendants – Sazerac Stitches

Office

Rug – CB2

Pendant Light – Matteo Lighting

Sofa – American Leather

Desk – Restoration Hardware

Main Bedroom

Floral Print Bedding – Spoonflower

Quilt – Crane and Canopy

Nightstands – Celadon Home

Lamps – West Elm

Chandelier – Museo Lighting

Grasscloth Wallpaper – Scalamandre

Main Bedroom Hallway

Runner – Loloi

Mirror – Arhaus

Flushmount Lights – CB2

Main Bathroom

Rug – Revival Rugs

Mirrors – Pottery Barn

Library

Curtain Panels – Spoonflower

Lamps – Hudson Valley Lighting

Sofas – Restoration Hardware

Sconces – Savoy House

Boy's Room

Rug – Loloi

Bed – World Market

Quilt and Lumbar Pillow – Target

Leopard Pillows – Pottery Barn

Curtain Panels – Two Pages Curtains

Girl's Room

Rug – Anthropologie

Bed – World Market

Quilt – Walmart

Leopard Pillows – Spoonflower

Lumbar Pillow – Urban Outfitters

Floor Lamp – Walmart

Lace Curtains – Amazon

Velvet Curtain Panels – Anthropologie

Chandelier – Miles Redd for Ballard Designs

Mirror – CB2

Doors

The doorknobs throughout our home are from Grandeur Hardware.

Acknowledgments

To my *Our Fifth House* blog readers, thank you for always encouraging me and helping me believe that I could inspire others to create unique spaces filled with personality despite not having a degree in interior design. Without you, this book would not exist. I will forever be grateful for your kindness, excitement, and support!

To Heather, thank you for believing in me and helping me make this dream a reality. And to the team at Harvest House, thank you for your dedication in making this book.

To my mom, thank you for showing me how to walk confidently to the beat of my own drum and how to value and appreciate my unique style. I'm finally appreciative of the countless hours of my childhood you spent dragging me along to antique malls, thrift stores, and garage sales.

To my dad, thank you for being a fix-it man and believing your daughter could be a fix-it woman. Thank you for teaching me how to ride a bike and for coming with me to the hardware store when I bought my compound miter saw.

To my family and friends, thank you for teasing me about bunny fairies. You keep me humble, and I appreciate you. I will never love my home more than when you are visiting.

To Kim, your incredible photography skills brought this book to life! Thank you so much for agreeing to do this with me!

To Brad, thank you for always trusting my process and cheering me on no matter how long a project takes, even when it means living with a toilet in the entry foyer for a couple of weeks. To Collin and Josie, creating a home for you has been the joy of my life! No matter where life takes you, our home will always be yours.

About the Author

Carmel Phillips is the creative founder and writer behind the DIY design blog *Our Fifth House,* where, since 2010, she has been encouraging readers to make their home their happy place. She believes that creating a home should be fun, not complicated, and the only design rule she follows is that a home should reflect the personality of the people who live under its roof.

As a wife and mom currently living in the Lowcountry of South Carolina, when she's not nose deep in a book or dreaming about her next design project, she enjoys collecting shells on the beach and riding her bike under the mossy oaks throughout her neighborhood.

For more inspiration,
connect with and follow Carmel at

www.ourfifthhouse.com
Instagram @ourfifthhouse

Cover design by Faceout Studio, Elisha Zepeda
Interior design by Faceout Studio, Paul Nielsen
Photography by Kim Graham Photography
Interior images © Pics Garden (zebra), KED 44 (leopard) / Shutterstock
Chart on page 31 informed by https://platt.edu/blog
/psychology-color-graphic-design/

 TEN PEAKS PRESS is a federally registered trademark of the Hawkins Children's
LLC. Harvest House Publishers, Inc., is the exclusive licensee of this trademark.

If These Walls Could Talk

Copyright © 2025 by Carmel Phillips
Published by Ten Peaks Press, an imprint of Harvest House Publishers
Eugene, Oregon 97408

ISBN 978-0-7369-9073-8 (hardcover)
ISBN 978-0-7369-9074-5 (eBook)

Library of Congress Control Number: 2024950112

Printed in China

25 26 27 28 29 30 31 32 33 / LP / 10 9 8 7 6 5 4 3 2 1

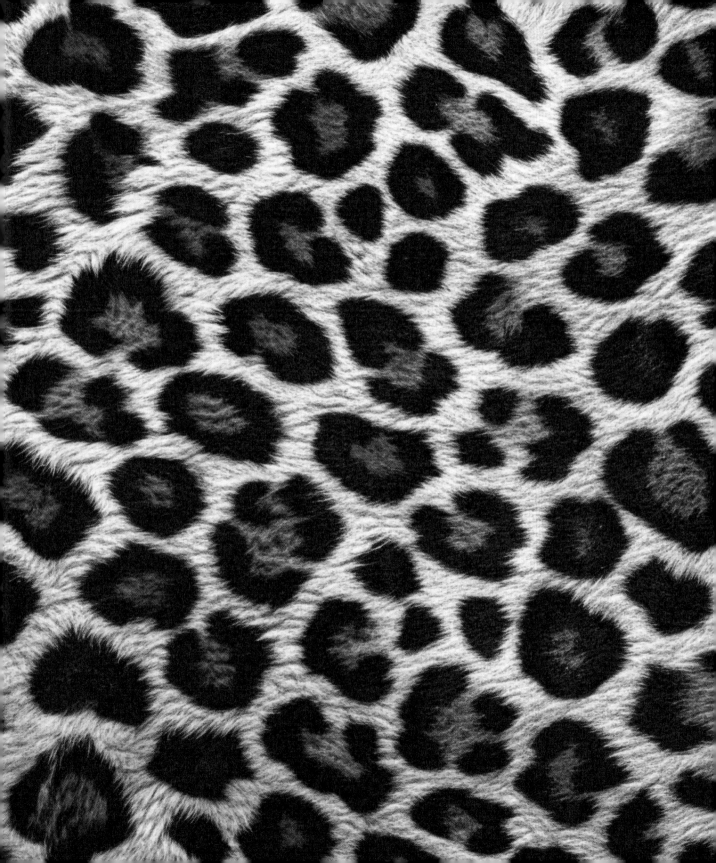

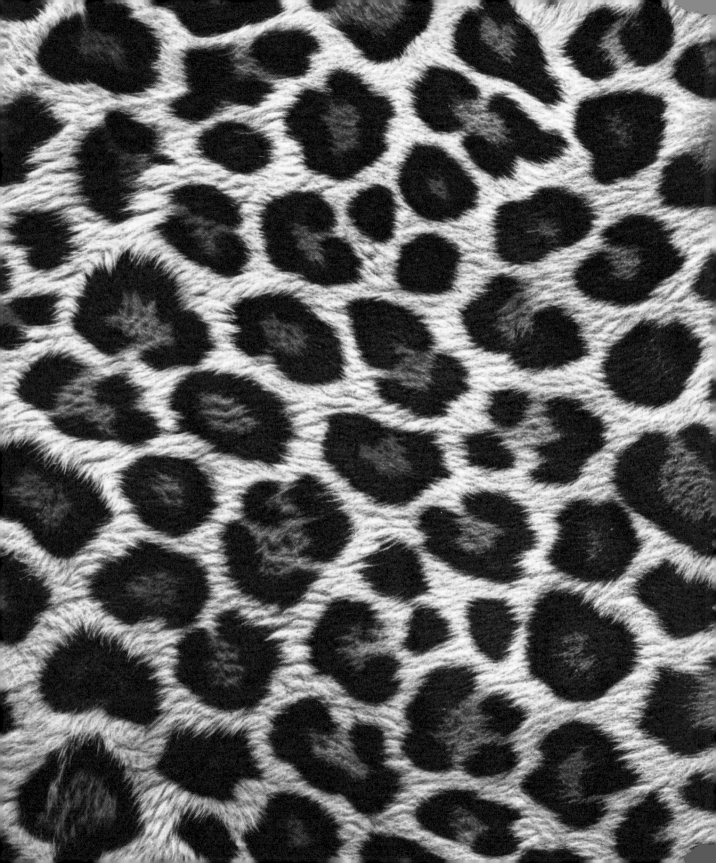